THE POWER OF
YOU!

How to Manifest the Life You Want

DR SCOTT ZARCINAS

OTHER BOOKS BY SCOTT ZARCINAS

Non-fiction
Being YOU! (*Your Natural State of Being)
The Banana Trap
It's Up to YOU!

Fiction
Samantha Honeycomb
The Golden Chalice
DeVille's Contract
Ananda
Roadman

THE POWER OF
YOU!

How to Manifest the Life You Want

DR SCOTT ZARCINAS

DoctorZed
Publishing
www.doctorzed.com

Copyright © Scott Zarcinas 2023

All rights reserved. No part of this book may be used or reproduced by any means, graphic, electronic, or mechanical, including photocopying, recording, taping or by any information storage retrieval system without the written permission of the publisher except in the case of brief quotations embodied in critical articles and reviews.

Copies of this book can be ordered via the author's website at www.scottzarcinas.com, booksellers or by contacting:

DoctorZed Publishing
10 Vista Ave, Skye,
South Australia 5072
www.doctorzed.com

ISBN: 978-0-6456384-4-8 (hc)
ISBN: 978-0-6456384-5-5 (sc)
ISBN: 978-0-6456384-6-2 (e)

A CiP number is available at the National Library of Australia.

Knee jerk or patella tendon reflex image © Aldona Griskeviciene | dreamstime.com

Because of the dynamic nature of the Internet, any web addresses or links contained in this book may have changed since publication and may no longer be valid. The views expressed in this work are solely those of the author and do not necessarily reflect the views of the publisher, and the publisher hereby disclaims any responsibility for them.

The author of this book does not dispense medical advice or prescribe the use of any technique as a form of treatment for physical, emotional, or medical problems without the advice of a physician, either directly or indirectly. The intent of the author is only to offer information of a general nature. In the event you use any of the information in this book for yourself, which is your constitutional right, the author and the publisher assume no responsibility for your actions.

DoctorZed Publishing rev. date: 12/02/2023

CONTENTS

Acknowledgements		vii
Letter to Abigail		viii
Introduction		**1**
Part I	**The Power of You**	**25**
Chapter 1	As You Think	27
Chapter 2	The Right Mindset	45
Chapter 3	Imagination, Intention & Attitude	63
Chapter 4	Identity, Purpose & Conviction	95
Part II	**Power Habit #1: Self-Assuredness & Self-Belief**	**105**
Chapter 5	The Power of Faith	107
Chapter 6	Certainty & Knowing	123
Part III	**Power Habit #2: Courage & Confidence**	**145**
Chapter 7	The Power of Belief	147
Chapter 8	The Power of Persistence	163
Part IV	**Power Habit #3: Other People Thinking**	**177**
Chapter 9	The Power of Service	179
Chapter 10	The Golden Rule	195
Part V	**Power Habit #4: Planning, Preparation & Perseverance**	**215**
Chapter 11	The Power of Commitment	217
Chapter 12	Daring to Dream	241
The Last Word		**273**
Further Reading		**276**

For every seeker—may you find your inner power.

ACKNOWLEDGEMENTS

To my wife, Martie, for your continual love and devotion. Leonie McKeon and Nicola Lipscombe, for your continuing support in what I'm trying to achieve. Last, but never least, my wonderful daughters, Zsa Zsa and Zenya, through you I learn more about love and the wonders of life every day.

Letter to Abigail

One moment makes the difference. Just a one moment. Such appears to be the extreme and undisputed power of a single moment.

We live in a world of appearance, Abigail, where the reality lies beyond the appearances, and this is also only what appears to be such powerful when in actuality it is not.

I realised that the power of the moment is not in the moment itself. The power, actually, is in us. Every single one of us has the power to make and shape our own moments. It is us who by feeling joyful, celebrate for a moment of success; and it is also us who by feeling saddened, cry and mourn over our losses. I, with all my heart and mind, now embrace this power which lies within us.

I wish life offers you more time to make use of this power. Remember, we are our own griefs, my dear, we are our own happinesses and we are our own remedies. Take care!

—Huseyn Raza

INTRODUCTION

ADMIT ONE: THE 5% CLUB

HAVE YOU EVER known anyone to ask for tips on how to fail?

Sounds silly, doesn't it? But there's a reason no self-help gurus are making millions on handing out their secrets of failure. That'd be an oxymoron.

Certainly no-one has written a book on the secrets to failure as far as I'm aware. Who would want to read it?

It seems most of us already know how to fail. We're already pretty good at it, so we don't need any advice on how to take failure to the next level. It would take someone with a confused sense of self to want to fail even more than he or she already was, or even more efficiently than what he or she was already doing.

For most of us, failure is par for the course. It's almost a natural human tendency. It's success that isn't normal.

In fact, it's estimated that for every 20 babies that are born in the Western world, only one of them will be deemed 'successful' at the age of 65 years. That's a mere 5% of the population.

That means the absolute majority of those babies, a staggering 19 out of 20, will grow up, get an education, maybe get a job, get married, start a family, and retire 65 years later without having made a so-called 'success' of their life. From the statistics, you could very well make this assumption:

Life has a 5% success rate.

Which is why we tend to seek out those who are successful and ask them what their secret to success is. We want to know what they did so we can replicate it and become part of The 5% Club who are successful and thriving.

SURVIVING VS THRIVING

No matter what time period in history, there have always been two types of people in this world: those who are surviving, and those who are thriving. This has only been magnified by recent world events, including the COVID pandemic of 2020-2022.

Those who are just surviving are barely keeping their heads above water, just trying to breathe and make it through to the next day. The bills mount up. Time is against them. Nothing seems to work. Life is something that happens to them, not for them. They feel constantly overwhelmed and inundated, barely able to make ends meet. Every day is the same as the day before, a struggle they feel will never end. Worse, the weeks, months, and years ahead will probably be a replica of what has gone before. They fear that this is their lot in life, that no matter what they do everything will remain as it is, a life with nothing but problems and no solutions.

Or they feel like hamsters on a wheel, running, running, running, doing so much work but not actually moving forward or getting ahead, simply getting exhausted and burning out. Not only are they barely surviving to live, they are, for all intents and purposes, merely living to survive.

But those who are thriving are the complete opposite. They work smarter, not harder. They don't just do things right, they do the right things, which makes them effective and successful. They are growing and expanding, even in the face of negative conditions. They feel strong, they feel safe, they feel creative, they feel energised, they feel free. The world is their oyster.

But there's another identifiable type between surviving and thriving, and these are the people who are reviving. They're finally emerging out of their struggles and difficulties, but they're not thriving just yet, and neither are they barely surviving. They are delicately balanced. Like saplings hesitantly poking through the ground, they are still quite delicate and vulnerable. Their uncertainty means they can either slip back into survival mode

INTRODUCTION

or, with the right nurturing, they can grow and thrive. They are full of potential, but as yet it is not fully realised.

Then again, there are others who are actually in a situation worse than surviving, and they are the ones who are diving. They are either on a slow, slippery slope downward, or they are spiralling and plunging downward. The days hold no joy. Life is futile. There is no light at the end of the tunnel. They are almost ready to give up.

These people need help just to even survive. To use a medical analogy, they need to stop the bleeding, otherwise they'll bleed out and perish if nothing is done. Once the bleeding has stopped, then they can recover and move back into survival mode. Which is actually a better place than where they are right now.

And then there are those who are on the complete opposite side of the spectrum, the ones who are doing even better than thriving—these people are jiving.

Where those who are diving or surviving live in a world of projected fear of life, those who are jiving live in a creative expression of love for life. They are growing exponentially. Every day gets better and better. They succeed for all the right reasons. They serve the advancement and development of all humanity, and they desire nothing more than for everyone on the planet to have life and have it abundantly. They care about others, they want to be part of 'something bigger', they are happy, productive, effective, and loving. They fully embrace life, with all its ups and downs, grabbing it with both hands and running with it as far as it will take them. Live happens for them, not to them.

These people have 'I Am Success' written across their foreheads. They are life members of The 5% Club and are the envy of all other people.

THE POWER OF YOU!

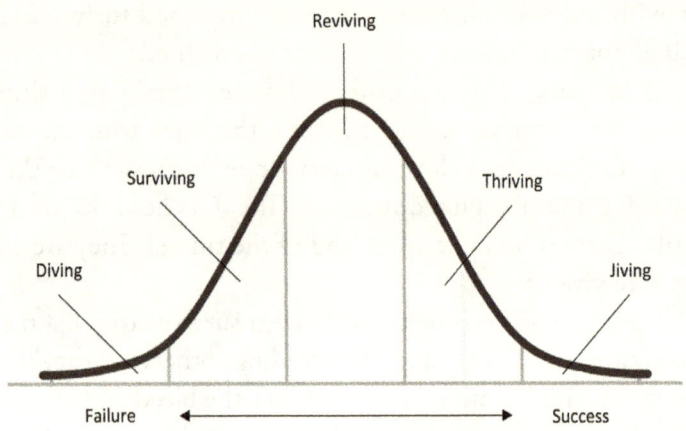

FIGURE 1:   Diving to Jiving Spectrum

But take note: your position on this diving-to-jiving spectrum doesn't determine your degree of success. Your progress does.

It isn't your current socio-economic status that determines your success. It's your determination to work your way forward and improve. It doesn't matter where you start. Whether you feel you are 'diving' and are working to progress to the level of 'surviving', or you feel you're 'reviving' and are working to progress to the level of 'thriving', it's the intention, effort, and momentum forward that is important. This is what counts. This is what determines your success. To be better today than yesterday, to be better tomorrow than today.

Conversely, your lack of intention, your refusal to put in any effort, and the slide backward through these levels, will be reflected in your failure to progress. But even if you feel you're sliding backwards, you can always arrest the slide and focus on what needs to be done to reverse the moment back in your favour.

How do you reverse the slide? How do you reverse your fortune? How do you end up jiving as a member of The 5% Club?

By claiming your own success.

INTRODUCTION

THE 4 TENETS OF SUCCESS

The problem many have with success is that it is elusive and unobtainable. No matter how hard we work, no matter how hard we try, it can seem that the grass is always greener on the other side of the fence. Despite all the effort we've put in over the years, it can seem as though others have success come their way easier.

It is constantly frustrating when success is always out of your reach. The frustration is compounded by the waiting. Getting rewarded for your efforts and hard work seems to take an eternity. Your patience begins to wane. Your faith is tested. Your resolve is weakened. You begin to think it will never happen for you.

It's normal to feel this way when we live in a world of instant everything—instant food, instant coffee, instant relationships, instant billionaires. When the whole world wants it now, so do we. This includes instant success.

Ultimately, there are two ways to view your life situation:

1. You can either *compare* yourself to others and burn yourself out by continually competing with them and trying to keep up with them, or
2. You can *ignore* what others are doing and focus on what you can do.

This means you can either keep looking with envy at the greener grass on the other side of the fence, or you can stop looking and focus on how you can make the grass greener on your side.

But what does that actually look like? Would you recognise success if you saw it?

It's worth a moment to consider, because I can bet a few dollars on the assumption that what success looks like to me isn't what success looks like to you. For me, success is a never-ending vista of golf courses as far as the eye can see. That's paradise, pure bliss. But to others, that's the very definition of hell, to be avoided at all costs.

Not that either perspective is more right than the other, just that our definitions of success and happiness are subjective and therefore different.

Which is the way it should be. You can't live somebody else's life, and you shouldn't even try to. You can't base your career, relationships, health, wealth, and wellbeing on somebody else's opinion of what success is. Not if you want to be happy and fulfilled. Not if you want your grass to be greener on your side of the fence.

You must claim your own success. You must define your own success and what that looks like. This is the foundation of success, of which there are 4 Tenets:

> Tenet #1: Success is Self-Prescribed
> Tenet #2: Success Comes Through You, Not to You
> Tenet #3: Success is a Habit
> Tenet #4: Success is a Side-Effect of Your Commitment to Your Life Purpose

Let's briefly discuss these four tenets now.

Tenet #1

The first of The 4 Tenets of Success, *Success is Self-Prescribed*, means you shouldn't rely on others or society to tell you what they think success for you should be. Nobody else knows you like you do. Only you know what success looks like from your point of view.

Success, therefore, is a personal brand. It's a personal brand that you must choose for yourself. Otherwise it's somebody else's personal brand, not yours.

Be deaf, then, to what others tell you is best. Take ownership of who you want to be and what you want to do, and define how success looks for you.

Nobody else can do that. Nobody else should do that.

Only you.

INTRODUCTION

Tenet #2

The Second Tenet of Success states that *Success Comes Through You, Not to You.*

There's a 'U' in success for a reason—success comes through you, not to you.

So don't try to be anything other than you. Don't try to be somebody else. Don't even try to be 'a success'.

Because success, even greatness, is first built on the foundation of *you*. If the first tenet of success is defining what success looks like, then the second tenet is defining who you are and choosing who you want to be.

Success begins with choosing it. It begins with the statement, "I am successful." First, in your mind, you choose to be successful, by identifying with success, and then what you do becomes an expression of who you state you are internally, a success. With this perspective, even mistakes, errors, miscalculations, setbacks, and failures become mere stepping-stones to the ultimate expression of your success, not major obstacles.

Therefore, make your foundation—your *you*—a rock on which to build your success.

Tenet #3

The Third Tenet of Success acknowledges that *Success is a Habit.*

Success isn't a secret treasure waiting for you to stumble upon. Success isn't the pot of gold at the end of the rainbow. Success is an act of creation, and any type of winning, any type of achievement, any type of development, is created through a process—a process of hard work, determination and unyielding will—which is why it's also a habit. Success is a habit of right being, right thinking, and right action.

This third tenet is the core theme of this book. The aim is to show you that, like scaling a mountain, your dreams are achieved in small steps, not large leaps. It's your habits that keep you moving toward your goals. Your habits create your momentum. Without good habits, you slow down and eventually stop the climb. So we need to break old habits that aren't serving you well and build good habits that will work for you, not against you.

As such, the intention of this book is to help you set your foundation for success through habits that will build your identity, purpose, and conviction. When you have clarity in who you are (identity), when you understand your role (purpose), and you are confident you are heading in the right direction (conviction), you have a tried and tested recipe for success:

- -> *Identity*: Who are you? Who do you want to be? What is your relationship to the world around you? Who and what do you identify with?
- -> *Purpose*: Why do you want to be that person? What is your intention? What it the meaning behind what you do? Why does it matter?
- -> *Conviction*: Where are you going? When do you want to arrive? How are you going to get there?

The clarity of your answers to these questions will be a predictive indication on your future success. As such, The 4 Power Habits that we will be discussing throughout this book are designed to help you achieve clarity on these three essential components—Identity, Purpose, Conviction. These 4 Power Habits are:

Power Habit #1: Self-Assuredness and Self-Belief

Power Habit #2: Courage and Confidence

Power Habit #3: Other People Thinking

Power Habit #4: Planning, Preparation & Perseverance

These 4 Power Habits derive from the principle that, when it comes to your success, habits of being are far more impactful and effective than habits of doing. They follow the 80:20 Rule and

INTRODUCTION

emphasise the importance of 'being success' (80% internal habits) over and above 'doing success' (20% external habits). These habits will be summarised in just a moment, then discussed in much greater detail.

Tenet #4

The Fourth Tenet of Success recognises that *Success is a Side-Effect of Your Commitment to Your Life-Purpose*.

To focus solely on outward success is to focus on a constantly moving target, a target that is very difficult to hit. But when your focus is on becoming the person you were born to be—your Life-Purpose—success is a natural outcome of that focus.

This is why, when you set goals, you should do it for the right reasons. Not to attain money, or possessions, or positions of power, but to use your goals to become that which you are capable of becoming. The best reason to set goals is not as destinations to arrive at, but as the *means* by which you grow into the person you always wanted to be and always thought you could. That's the real value of outward achievement and success. That it is the conduit by which you express who you really are—the best version of yourself.

When you use goals in this manner, what you do externally becomes an outward expression of who you are being internally. Success, therefore, begins with *vision*, the crystal-clear impression of who you are and who you want to be. What you do, how you act, demonstrates that vision of who you are and want to be, a visible expression of your mental impression.

This is especially so when you commit to your Life Purpose, when you commit to your reason for being. Mark Twain said the two most important days of your life are the day you were born, and the day you find out why. When you seek and find out the greater reason you were born, you discover something really important—you discover your Life Purpose. You discover your reason for why you are here and now.

Why is this so important? Because the fount of success flows forth from the inside. We know this from the Second Tenet of Success, that success comes through you, not to you. When your Life Purpose becomes your life's expression and you commit to it, you can then make clearer choices on who you are being and what you want to become. You get to decide who and what you are. Surely there is no greater success than that?

On the flipside, if you don't make that decision, if you put off making that choice, what you do will flow from that lack of focus and become the expression of that lack. Eventually you will lose momentum and progress, and you will grind to stagnation. You will not reach your goal because you have not reached yourself.

Your success, therefore, depends on your commitment to who you want to be.

THE 4 POWER HABITS OF SUCCESS

As previously mentioned, the aim of this book is to help you break old habits that aren't serving you well and to help you develop four powerful habits that will gain you entry into The 5% Club. These habits will take your life to the next level. Sections II, III, IV, and V will deal specifically with a single Power Habit and the tools you need to develop each one, but for now here is a summary of the 4 Power Habits of Success.

Power Habit #1: Self-Assuredness and Self-Belief

The first Power Habit builds on the principle that success comes to those who do not allow self-consciousness or past failures to get in their way. Why? Because failure is not the end unless you allow it to be.

This habit embraces the attitude that failures are just stepping-stones to your success. Failure is not to be avoided. Rather, you must learn to accept it as an integral part of your success. Failure

INTRODUCTION

is not something to keep you being stuck. Instead, you must learn that success is waiting for you to meet it halfway.

How do you accept failure? How do you keep moving forward despite failing?

By deliberately and intentionally developing the habit of unshakable self-assuredness—the certitude that, despite any setbacks, you will be steadfast in who you are, what you do, why you do it, and how you do it.

Identity. Purpose. Conviction. These will be your power tools of success.

Power Habit #2: Courage and Confidence

The second Power Habit gives you the tools to overcome the biggest obstacle to your success—fear.

As the saying goes, a ship in the harbour is safe, but that's not what ships are made for. A ship is made for sailing. Which means a ship and all its crew must eventually leave the safety of the harbour and venture forth into the unknown. On ancient maps prior to the discovery of the new worlds, cartographers would draw fearsome dragons and sea monsters in the uncharted waters at the edge of the known world. They would caption these fearsome creatures with, "Here there be monsters!"

Of course there were no such monsters, but how did the ancient sailors know that if they didn't go there and take a look? What monsters lurk in the unchartered waters of your life? What monsters are keeping you moored in your safe harbour, too afraid to sail forth to your new world?

The unknown can be frightening. The unknown can fill you so full of dread and anxiety that you do not dare leave your safe harbour. But that's not what you are made for.

Fears never go away, so that just leaves you with two choices: stay safe in your harbour, or hoist your sails and learn to navigate around those fears. What do you choose?

If you choose the first option, you won't need to do anything other than stay where you are. If you choose the second option, this second Power Habit will help you to navigate around your fears and progress toward success. It will help you develop the absolute confidence in your abilities to overcome any challenge that stands in your way. It will help you to harness the courage of the ancient sailors to take action in spite of any fears that assail you, to sail toward your destiny.

Power Habit #3: Other People Thinking

The third Power Habit follows the Golden Rule of doing unto others that which you would have them do unto you.

Why? Because success flows from collaboration, not from competition. This is the principle of 'givers gain', whereby the more you give unto others, the more you get back. Where the hand that sows is the hand that reaps the harvest. Collaborative success means more people succeed, more people win, more people are happy. It is not bound by any competitive restraints and is therefore unconstrained and unlimited. Competitive success, though, is by definition confined to only those on the winning side. It requires a winner and a loser, which limits it to the individual or the group that is deemed the victor.

The game of Monopoly is an example of competitive, and therefore limited, success. Once a player owns all the property and all the houses and all the hotels on the board, the game is over. The other players become bankrupt. They can do nothing else but leave and go and play another game. The winner sits alone with all her money and nobody left to play with. Where's the fun in that?

But imagine if the game of Monopoly was played with a collaborative mindset, not a competitive mindset. Imagine if each player looked for win-win solutions and viewed every moment in the game as an opportunity to serve and create value for the other

INTRODUCTION

players. Imagine if each player's ambition was to find out what other people needed and then helped them to fill that need.

Imagine if everyone celebrated everyone else's success as their own success.

Power Habit #4: Planning, Preparation & Perseverance

The fourth Power Habit follows the maxim that the process is more important than the result. Why? Because the process is the only thing that can be done in this moment and the result is still in the future: *the process leads to the result.*

If money is your goal, then to make money you need to invest money. If peace and love is your goal, then the way to that goal is through peace and love. If you want to have a great relationship with another person, you need to have a great relationship with yourself.

Money is the method and practice to make more money. Peace and love is the method and practice to attain peace and love. Being a wonderful friend to yourself is the method and practice to have wonderful friendships with others.

In other words, the pathway to your success is established by whatever that success looks like and feels like to you. The destination sets the means by which you arrive at that destination. The result determines the process by which you attain that result.

The key is commitment to the process. Earl Nightingale, a motivational speaker and the bestselling author of *The Strangest Secret*,[1] was considered the father of modern-day personal development. In the 1950s he was one of the first authors to put his books to audiotape and LP record, selling millions of copies and thus creating the 'learning through listening' industry. Nightingale spoke at lengths about success and being successful, and that every person who knows what he wants knows what he must become. He

---

[1] *The Strangest Secret: How to live the life you desire*, Earl Nightingale, Nightingale Conant, 1957 (audio)

also emphasised that success was not an end in itself, like a target to hit, but a process, and he defined success as the 'progressive realisation of a worthy ideal'.

To break Nightingale's definition into its parts, one of the primary elements of success is that it is 'progressive'—it's moving forward, expanding, enlarging. Success, therefore, is *growth*.

The next element of success, according to Nightingale, is that it is also a 'realisation'—the manifestation of that which you have sought to be and do. It is an unfolding, a bringing into material reality and physical form that which was once only in thought form.

The final element of Nightingale's definition of success is that it also has to be 'worthy'—it has to have *value*, not only to you, but to others, to your community, to the world. It has to mean something to others. It can't be gained from lies. It can't be gained from cheating others. It can't be gained from taking what isn't yours. Your success is worthy because of the worth you give to the world.

What Nightingale's definition of success is hinting at, is that *result and process are one*. What separates them is the flow time. In that time, you plan, you prepare, and you persevere—you commit to the process. You take proper care in planning for what you want and prepare for any eventuality. If you persist, the results will come. But to focus too much on the result is to lose sight of the path and thus lose your direction.

So focus on the process now to achieve the results you want in the future.

HAPPINESS

Fortune and success take many forms, and one of the most enjoyable forms is the deep sense of happiness and joy. You can therefore replace the word success with happiness so that The 4 Tenets of Success now become 'The 4 Tenets of Happiness':

INTRODUCTION

Tenet #1: Happiness is Self-Prescribed
Tenet #2: Happiness Comes Through You, Not to You
Tenet #3: Happiness is a Habit
Tenet #4: Happiness is a Side-Effect of Your Commitment to Your Life Purpose

Happiness, though, isn't pleasure. Pleasure is tied to its opposite, which is pain. Deep seated happiness is a permanent state of being, a joy of life that isn't tied to any opposites, like sadness, because it is rooted in the essence of who you are, which simply *is*. It is a joy that can weather any storm. It is not dependent on how much money you have. It isn't dependent on how many houses, cars, diamond rings, designer clothes, fancy shoes, or in fact any possessions you own. It isn't dependent on what you do, your career, your academic achievements, your position in society. It isn't dependent on your family, your relationships, your friendships, your attractiveness, your physical attributes.

Happiness isn't dependent on anything external to you. It is dependent only on you.

The American creator of the Living Love method, personal growth author and lecturer, Ken Keyes Jr., affirmed the truth of happiness in his book, *The Handbook to Higher Consciousness*:[2]

> *Happiness is there, waiting inside of you... It is, indeed, and inside job.*

It is therefore incumbent on you to define your own happiness (Tenet #1). You must choose what happiness means for you. You must decide on what happiness looks like, feels like, sounds like. Until you decide, happiness waits inside for you to choose it.

---

[2] *The Handbook to Higher Consciousness*, Ken Keys Jr., Living Love Center, 1975

Then, once you've chosen it, happiness can be demonstrated and expressed through you (Tenet #2). Think of happiness as money in your bank account. Whatever the total amount of money in your account happens to be, from a few dollars to a few thousand dollars, or even more, the money sitting in that account is just a number. It can't be experienced or 'felt' until it is spent. You can only experience the spending power of those funds when you release those funds. Until you spend the money, it is only a potential waiting for you to choose it. Only once it's spent can you 'feel' what it's like to have that money.

The same with happiness. The only difference is that money is finite, happiness is infinite—when you spend money it diminishes; when you spend happiness it expands and grows.

> *You can run out of money, but you can never run out of happiness because happiness is who you are.*

Money, possessions, and power are perishable crowns. They come and they go. You place them on your head only to have them vanish into thin air. But happiness isn't perishable. Just like the magic pudding, the magic of happiness is that there is always more of it. Happiness is the gift that keeps on giving. You have an unlimited supply of happiness in your 'happiness account', and it patiently waits for you to spend it. This you do by sharing it. Until you do, until you share freely and without condition, it is only a potential waiting for you to choose it. Only then, only once it's shared, can you experience and feel what it's like to be happy.

It can't be any other way. That's why you can't feel anyone else's happiness. Even when you are laughing with your friends, each person is just sharing their own happiness. Nobody is feeling another's happiness. Each is 'spending' their happiness and experiencing what their limitless happiness account feels like when they share it.

INTRODUCTION

It's also why you can't 'get' happiness from somebody else. Other people can't 'make you happy'. Possessions can't make you happy either. Neither can a job, or a holiday. Neither can money. We all know of millionaires who are miserable and unhappy, and we all know of people in poverty who are happy and fulfilled, so it isn't external circumstances that is the magic pill for everlasting happiness. Only internal circumstances can give you happiness. Or more precisely, only internal circumstances can release the happiness that is waiting for you to choose it. If external circumstances do anything, it is only to help you make the choice for happiness that's already there inside you.

But you really don't need external circumstances to make that choice. That's already in your power.

So why not make it a habit (Tenet #3) to choose happiness? Why not set your intention to focus on your happiness account and commit to sharing it? Why not make the decision a thousand times a day to be happy, irrespective of your current circumstances?

The problem for most people, and the reason why this choice is so hard to make, is that happiness has become conditional. "I'll only be happy when..." "I'll be happier if you don't do that... or if you would only do such a such..." "I'll be happier if I achieve a certain goal." "I'll be happy once I have a million dollars."

The list goes on and on. But any condition you put on your happiness is a block to sharing your happiness. Conditions set withdrawal limits on your happiness account, and thus limit your experience of happiness. Even if your football team is losing and you're not having much fun at all, you can still choose to be happy no matter the score line. Even if you're having an argument with your partner or with a family member and it's getting heated, you can still choose to remain calm, centred, and happy irrespective of what that person has done, or what they haven't done, to spark the argument.

It can be difficult in the heat of the moment to make this choice, but you can do it. It's not impossible, and it does become easier when you make it a habit. Remember what Huseyn Raza said in his *Letter to Abigail* at the front of this book:

> *Every single one of us has the power to make and shape our own moments. It is us who by feeling joyful, celebrate for a moment of success; and it is also us who by feeling saddened, cry and mourn over our losses. I, with all my heart and mind, now embrace this power which lies within us.*

You have the power to make and shape your own moments. All you need to do is manifest this power which lies within you, which you do by putting no conditions upon it.

Once your happiness is free of conditions, once it is recognised as unconditional, then it just becomes a choice of how you manifest that happiness. Having fun with your friends. Being kind and considerate to others. Giving a smile when all others seem to have forgotten how to smile. Lending a hand to those in need. Helping others how to find their own inner happiness. Listening to others with an open mind and a caring heart. Being patient when others are stressed and anxious. Not reacting with anger or frustration when somebody cuts you off in busy traffic.

The list goes on and on. You have the power to make and shape your own moments, and the 4 Power Habits is how you make this happen.

Happiness, like success, also arises when you commit to your Life Purpose (Tenet #4).

When you have a cause to which you believe in and commit yourself to, happiness is a by-product of that commitment. Happiness is a natural side-effect of striving for a meaningful cause,

INTRODUCTION

of knowing what you do has a beneficial effect for others, your community, your nation, even humanity.

Eleanor Roosevelt, former First Lady of the United States of America, penned these philosophical words in her book, *You Learn by Living*:[3]

> *Happiness is not a goal, it is a by-product. Paradoxically, the one sure way not to be happy is deliberately to map out a way of life in which one would please oneself completely and exclusively. After a short time, a very short time, there would be little that one really enjoyed. For what keeps our interest in life and makes us look forward to tomorrow is giving pleasure to other people.*

Happiness comes from knowing that what you do matters, despite the difficulties, despite the obstacles, despite the headwinds against you. On the flipside, when you don't have a cause to live and work for, when you are unsure about your purpose in life, the effect on your sense of being reflects that absence of purpose and meaning, which becomes the experience of futility, despair, cynicism, frustration, confusion, even fear, and anything but happiness.

Barak Obama, the 44th President of the United States of America, once said that you can only realise your true potential when you hitch your wagon to something bigger than yourself. That 'something bigger' is a great cause. Because when you have a great cause to live and work for, you realise a truly great effect—your true potential.

One part of your true potential is the permanent sense of personal happiness and wellbeing.

---

[3] *You Learn by Living: 11 Keys for a More Fulfilling Life*, Eleanor Roosevelt, Harper, 1960

YOUR SUCCESS, YOUR RESPONSIBILITY

You can summarise The 4 Tenets of Success and Happiness like this:

Your success and happiness begins and ends with you.

But so does your failure.

Which is a trap you must avoid, because The 4 Tenets of Success can just as easily be 'The 4 Tenets of Failure':

Tenet #1: Failure is Self-Prescribed

Tenet #2: Failure Comes Through You, Not to You

Tenet #3: Failure is a Habit

Tenet #4: Failure is a Side-Effect of Your Lack of Commitment to Your Life Purpose

Failure is self-prescribed (Tenet #1) when you allow others to define what success looks like for you. When you agree to someone else's definition of success, you automatically jump on the slippery slide to failure. This includes your parent's definition of success, your friends' definition, your peers' definition, even society's definition. Whenever you feel as though you need to keep up with the Joneses, you've bought into their definition of what success is for you. Whenever you feel you need to impress somebody, you've bought into their definition of what success is for you.

To quote again from Eleanor Roosevelt on the subject of integrity and fully living from the space of inner being:

> *When you adopt the standards and the values of someone else or a community or a pressure group, you surrender your own integrity. You become, to the extent of your surrender, less of a human being.*

INTRODUCTION

When you fail to define your own success and self-worth, you are abdicating your responsibility to define and prescribe your success and thus leave it in the hands of others, allowing them to determine who you are and what you should do. You sign your life away. You hand your power over to somebody else, somebody who most likely doesn't have your best intentions in mind. You lose your identity. You become less of a human being.

Nobody in The 5% Club has ever let anybody else define their success.

Failure comes through you, not to you (Tenet #2), because success does not depend on imitating the success of others. Failure does. Success does not arise from following in the path of someone else. Failure does.

Why? Because you cannot be them, no matter how hard you try. At best, you can only imitate them. But an imitation is just a poor copy, it is never the real thing; it is fool's gold. The reflection in the mirror can never be the person standing before the mirror, no matter how much they look alike. There is no substance in a forgery. Everyone knows it isn't the real thing. Everyone knows it's just a pretence.

So your success must come from being the real thing, the real you. It must come from finding that which is successful in you and following your own path.

Your own identity. Your own purpose. Your own conviction.

Like success, failure is also a habit (Tenet #3). The truly successful know this. They know that success isn't determined by the cards you are dealt, it is determined by how well you play them. They take responsibility for who they are, for what they want, and for how they act and behave.

They therefore take responsibility for all their successes, and all their failures too. They do not identify as a victim. They identify as a victor. They do not blame others for their failures. They accept what's happened and prepare for the next roll of the dice. They do not make excuses for their lack of achievement. They determine to set right what mistakes have been made in order to improve their odds of success the next time around.

I myself have often succumbed to habits of failure. I have fallen into the trap many times. One of the worst times was as a young adult, when I procrastinated for 15 years before I started writing my first book, *The Golden Chalice*.[4] As a 15-year-old high school student, all I wanted was to be a bestselling author like my heroes, Stephen King, Wilbur Smith, and John Irving. But an underlying fear of failure and rejection prevented me from even trying.

For the next 15 years after graduating from high school, I told everyone who'd listen that I was going to write a book. But I didn't. I procrastinated instead and made excuses as to why I couldn't write: too busy, too tired, too little time, not enough money, the wrong equipment. I dived into the blame game head first. I blamed circumstances. I blamed others. I blamed my job. I blamed anything and anybody except myself. I steadfastly refused to take responsibility for my own failures to write the book I had wanted to since high school.

I was well and truly in the habit of failure. The fear of not being good enough and the fear of rejection kept me there. My own fears. Nobody else's. What these fears told me was that if I didn't write, I couldn't fail; and if I didn't fail, I couldn't be rejected by others. But it was all a lie. A lie I totally believed in, a lie I told myself thousands of times a week. A lie I actively lived out.

The consequence of living out this lie was trapping myself in my own cage of untruths for many years. It was a prison sentence of my own making. I identified as a victim, which made me a prisoner in my own mind, and it wasn't until I was 30 that I was

---

[4] *The Golden Chalice: A Pilgrim's Chronicle*, Scott Zarcinas, DoctorZed Publishing, 2013

INTRODUCTION

able to finally escape my fears of failure and rejection and start writing. Procrastination fed my identity as a victim and it became a habit, an addiction-like habit of failure. It stole 15 years of my life, 15 years I can't get back. But I console myself that at least it wasn't 50 years of wasted opportunity, which it could well and truly have been if I'd continued to listen to the lies I was telling myself and remained trapped in my victim identity.

So do not repeat my mistake and do not identify with failure. Do not make failure a habit. The cost is a too high price to pay. Make success a habit instead.

Make success your identity, your purpose, your conviction.

Failure is also a side-effect of your lack of commitment to your Life Purpose (Tenet #4). Why? Because a life without a cause is a life without effect.

The parable of *The Priest and the Bricklayers* is an insightful story that highlights the impact of failing to embrace a cause to which you can 'hitch your wagon'. It goes like this:

> One day, a priest encountered three bricklayers enroute to his church.
>
> "What are you building?" he asked the first bricklayer.
>
> "I'm just laying bricks," the bricklayer said in annoyance.
>
> The priest moved on and asked the second bricklayer what he was building.
>
> "I'm building a wall," said the bricklayer, slightly more welcoming than the first bricklayer.
>
> The priest then asked the third bricklayer, "What are you building?"
>
> "I'm building a cathedral!" said the bricklayer, beaming with pride.

The first bricklayer the priest encountered had no real purpose in what he was doing. He was just laying bricks and couldn't wait to finish the job and be somewhere else. He was simply working to live. The second bricklayer had a minor purpose, to build a wall, but even then it was just a wall and it probably didn't matter what it was for. He didn't care for the purpose of the wall because he wasn't committed to any purpose himself. It was just a means to an end.

What both these bricklayers failed to realise was that they were limiting themselves and their experience of life, not by what they were doing, but by *why* they were doing it. They had fallen into the trap Barak Obama warned about, failing to live their true potential because of their poverty of ambition and asking too little of themselves. They had weak causes, and thus weak effects.

Here is the lesson of the first two bricklayers:

> *Your failure to identify a higher cause to which you can devote your efforts will inevitably result in a diminished sense of value of yourself and your work.*

The third bricklayer, however, was working for something much larger than himself. He approached his work with joy and enthusiasm. He wanted to be involved in building something of value to the community. He didn't want to be anywhere else other than where he was. He was dedicated to his cause. He lived to work. Not because of anything he received from doing the work, like a salary, but because of what he could give back to others by doing his work.

He was grateful to work, and his work was his legacy. The first two bricklayers were only working for what they could get or extract from it. Three bricklayers laying the same bricks and earning the same wage. Only one of them was a success.

That's why your success begins and ends with you (and your failure too).

PART I

THE POWER OF YOU

1 AS YOU THINK

THE 80:20 RULE

THE EMPHASIS ON success, happiness, and failure so far has been on identifying who you are being and much less on what you are doing. The fundamental principle underlying The 4 Power Habits is this: Get yourself right, get your mindset right, get your relationship with yourself right, and what you do will automatically be right.

First be right, then do right.

What this means is that success and happiness first result from following the process of being who you are, and then from expressing and manifesting that inner state through your actions. Being precedes doing. Being is cause and doing is effect. But in this physical world, physical achievement and success also requires physical action and effort. Which is why the manifestation of anything you want to experience is both being *and* doing.

Using the 80:20 Rule, if you consider success as an iceberg, then 20% of what success looks like is above the waterline—doing—and 80% of success is what you don't see below the waterline—being. The 20% 'doing' things that are observable include your knowledge and expertise, your skills and abilities, as well as your actions and behaviours, your results and achievements.

But the vast majority of success is unobservable and remains unseen to an outside observer. These are the 80% 'being' things, which includes your identity and character, your motivation and conviction. It includes your reason for being, your Life Purpose, the 'Why' of who you are and what you do. It includes your Imagination, Intention, and Attitude, three superpowers that we will discuss in great detail throughout this book. It includes your self-belief and assuredness, your mindset and perspective, your emotions and feelings. It includes your values, your morals, your ethics, your principles to which you hold yourself accountable. It also includes your spirituality, your ability to perceive your connection to your inner power, to others, to nature, to the world, to the universe, your ability to transcend and grow into the person you are capable of being.

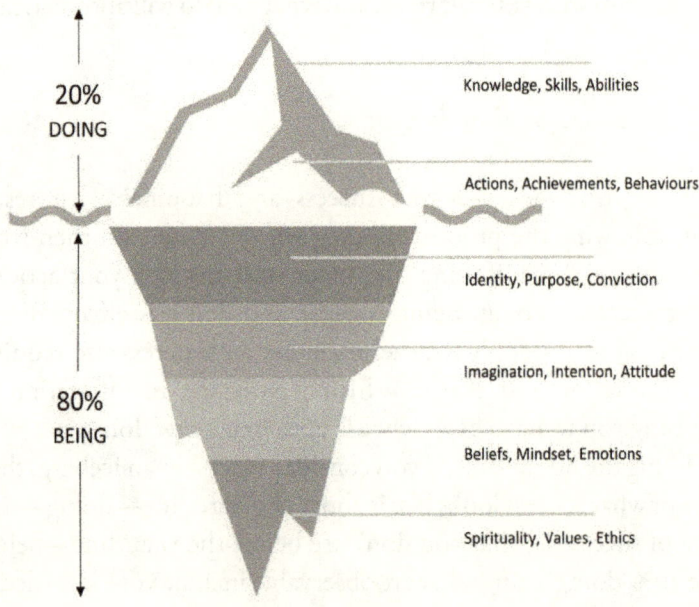

FIGURE 2:   Success is an Iceberg

The 80:20 Rule is therefore a good rule of thumb for using The 4 Power Habits, where 80% of their implementation is *being* and 20% of their implementation is *doing*. This is especially so for the manifestation of your success and happiness:

Success and happiness = 80% being + 20% doing

Yet, this is the antithesis of what society and our education systems have taught us, that success and happiness are the result of 80% doing (outer work) and 20% being (inner work). That's probably being generous: it's probably more like 99% doing and 1% being. Why? Because society equates success and happiness with getting and 'having', not being and sharing, and the only way you can 'have more' is to 'do more'.

So the accepted belief is that the more work you do, the harder you work, the more success and happiness you will achieve. "Do more to be more!" is the mantra. So we all do what everyone else is doing, never questioning this underlying principle that success comes to those who work themselves into the ground.

Yet, if success and happiness were more aligned with what you do than who you are being, then it follows that the more work you do and the faster you do it, the more 'success' you will achieve and the faster you will accomplish it. But that simply isn't what happens. Burn out, stress, anxiety, and mental health issues are worse in Western society than previous decades, not better. Despite advances in technology, despite how hard we work, despite the increasing number of hours and overtime we are doing, there is ample research to show that our collective sense of wellbeing is diminishing, not increasing. The world is not a happy place despite all our efforts to the contrary.

To follow society's mantra of "Do more to be more!", then, is akin to following the words of false prophets: you risk subjugating yourself to the power of others and enslaving yourself to their whims and desires. Your life is no longer your own.

So let's embrace a new mantra, "Be more to have more!" and reclaim what is rightfully ours, our *life*. Be more 'you' to have more success. Be more 'you' to have more happiness.

Let's embrace the 80:20 Rule of 80% being and 20% doing, and make this world a much better place for you and everyone you touch.

IT'S TIME YOU SHOWED UP

Doing, of course, is important. Just not as important as being.

Yet dreams without action are just wishes. Wishes don't achieve anything substantial. Wishful thinking doesn't initiate action, which means the things that need to get done get left undone. Only intentional thinking initiates action. You can't wish something into existence, but you can increase your chances by applying your will to it.

When you will something, as opposed to just wishing for it, you trigger a set of actions, behaviours, plans, and processes that work toward the achievement of your intention. You get the things done that need to be done. You finish the things you say you'll do. You don't leave a hundred things half-started and half-completed. You develop the successful habit of completing. You show up and do what you say you will do.

It's been said that, for the great majority of the time, being a success is as simple as just turning up. Actor, director, and comedian, Woody Allen, once quipped that showing up is 80% of life. If that's so, the equivalent of what 'showing up' is to your life is what finishing is to your success:

Finishing is 80% of success.

Whether you're an employee or an employer, you've probably noticed that the main difference between the colleague who is always considered for promotion and the colleague who is left languishing at the same desk for years is, more often than not, *reliability*. Although promotional desirability is multifactorial, often political, and not necessarily based on any single character trait or skill level, the successful colleague can nevertheless be relied upon to get things done. The other colleague, although well-meaning and polite and, by all accounts, a nice person, can't be relied upon as readily.

No publisher ever published a manuscript only half-written. They may well buy the rights to publish an uncompleted work, but they certainly won't ask the printer to run off a few thousand copies while they wait for the author to complete the book. No, the manuscript has to be finished before it can be published.

New homeowners won't be allowed to move in (or wouldn't want to move in) to their newly purchased house until the house is complete. There would be no point moving in without a roof, electricity, plumbing, or furnishings. No, the house has to be finished before the homeowner can move in.

You wouldn't pay the taxi driver who stops halfway to your destination and tells you to get out and walk the rest of the way. No, like any mode of transport, your fare covers you for the completion of the journey.

Integral to any success is therefore completion. Finishing the job. This goes not only for publishing books, building houses, and transporting you to your destination, but for anything and everything you do. This includes at work, at home, in your relationships, your education, your health, your wellbeing, even your leisure and adventure activities.

Because if you have developed a habit of not finishing what you set out to do, you're like a hot air balloon weighted down with sandbags, unable to lift off and soar into the sky. All those half-completed and never-finished tasks hold you back. They are mental sandbags weighing you down and preventing you from being the person you are capable of being. They stop you from getting from where you are now to where you want to be.

William James, who is considered the father of American psychology in mid-19th Century, and one of the USA's greatest philosophers, observed that nothing is more exhausting than half-completed tasks. The mental weight of knowing you still have many things to finish is emotionally, physically, and psychologically draining.

But if you have a lot of half-completed tasks or endeavours, then this means you have at least *started*. There are many reasons for non-achievement, and by far one of the biggest reasons is the failure to begin. Procrastination, putting things off, being lazy, getting distracted, anything that stops you from rolling up your sleeves and starting on your project is the first hurdle you need to conquer before you can begin your journey of success.

The Chinese parable tells us that the journey of a thousand miles begins with the first step in the right direction. Beginning your journey to success is actually the hardest step. Sure, obstacles and setbacks will always occur along the way and hamper your ability to finish what you started, but if finishing is 80% of success, then starting is 20% of success.

THE 3 PITFALLS TO SUCCESS

Once you have started on your journey to success, you need to be aware of the all the pitfalls that might hinder your progress along your journey. Starting is hard, but so is finishing. If you have a lot of half-completed tasks and projects, you need to think about why you've put down your tools and walked away from the job. Is it the lack of commitment or motivation? Fear of failure? Self-criticism? Mental tiredness? Too much distraction? Lack of know-how? Overwhelmed?

All of the above?

Just as there are many obstacles getting in the way of getting started, there are just as many along the journey to completion. Yet there are generally three main pitfalls or reasons for failing to achieve what you set out to achieve, and they are all wired into your neural circuitry, your brain.

This means you can actually do something about them because the brain is not set in marble. It has a remarkable feature called neuroplasticity, which means the neural circuitry of your brain is not hardwired like the wiring of a house or a building. Rather, it is constantly changing and rewiring depending on what you set your mind to do.

We know this from stroke patients. Some patients with large strokes can lose the ability to walk or even talk. But over time with rehabilitation and treatment, their brain can rewire around the dead part of the brain and the patient can learn to walk and talk again. This can only happen because of the brain's neuroplasticity.

It's the same with learning new habits. The brain's neuroplasticity means it can rewire to learn complex tasks that were previously unable to be done. A child learning to walk is neuroplasticity at work. So is learning how to ride a bike, learning how to play the piano, learning a new language. Age is not a barrier. New habits can be achieved at any age. Which means you can use your brain's remarkable neuroplasticity to overcome old habits of failure and learn new habits of success.

Old habits die hard, but at least they can die. The reason they die hard is because they are integrated into your brain's neurocircuitry and embedded in your identity of who you think you are. So yes, sometimes letting old habits die to make room for new habits means you sometimes have to let a little bit of your identity die with them so that a new identity can resurrect from the ashes, like a Phoenix.

First, though, you need to understand why old habits are so embedded in your identity, and it has a lot to do with these three aspects of your being:

1. Your thoughts and beliefs.
2. Your emotions and feelings.
3. Your instinctive reactions and behaviours.

In one of his many quotes, Earl Nightingale said that as a 29-year-old, after years of searching for the secret to success, he found it in the pages of Napoleon Hill's book, *Think and Grow Rich*.[5] Just a few words, six in fact, but enough change his life and, by default, change the lives of millions of people who have read his books and listened to his audio productions:

We become what we think about.

For Nightingale, these words were prophetic. Yet, Nightingale realised, this insight wasn't new. The notion that with your thoughts you create your world had been passed down for thousands of years through the words and writings of the prophets and philosophers:

As ye think, so shall ye be.

Neville Goddard, bestselling author of *Feeling is the Secret*, was one of the earliest proponents of the New Thought movement in the USA, whose works, albeit controversial, have influenced millions around the world. In his book, *Awakened Imagination and the Search*,[6] Goddard spoke about the power of your thoughts and how instrumental they are in determining your experience in life. *Who* you are in your inner world is *what* you are in your outer world, as he put it.

Your outward world is a reflection of your inner world, a mirror of what is going on inside your mind. Your inner world is powerful. Your thoughts are powerful, probably more than you realise.

You are powerful, probably more than you realise.

How you think is how you will become. That is your power.

---

[5] *Think and Grow Rich*, Napoleon Hill, The Ralston Society, 1937

[6] *Awakened Imagination and the Search*, Neville Goddard, G. & J. Publishing, 1954

THE POWER OF THOUGHT

Your thoughts and beliefs are powerful. With your thoughts you gain identity, you gain purpose, you gain conviction.

Everything begins with how you think, and the spring from which all your thoughts arise is that part of your mind we call your imagination. Imagination, therefore, is first cause—first you think, then you feel, then you act. As such, your thoughts can either work for you or against you. They can either help you soar like a hot air balloon to the destination of your dreams, or they can anchor you down like sandbags.

You know this in your own experiences. Think of a time when you really wanted something. For example, a car, a house, a holiday, a course to further your education. You had a vision of what you wanted, a goal you wanted to achieve. You probably thought about that car, that house, that holiday, that course all the time. While you were at work, while you were at home. While you were even sleeping. You probably thought about how you were going to afford it. You probably thought of all the ways you could save the money or borrow the money, and then you worked out a plan to pay for it.

Then you did it. You got what you wanted; and you got it through constant thinking about it, then getting motivated and enthusiastic about it, then taking action on getting it. That's how it worked for you in the past, and that's how it will work for you now and in the future—thinking, feeling, acting.

But just as your thoughts got you what you wanted in the past, they can also work the other way. If you're not careful, your own thoughts can prevent you from getting what you want and severely curtail your successes. Instead of thinking about all ways you could save money or borrow money to pay for your car, house, holiday, or educational course, imagine if you spent all your time thinking about why you couldn't get what you wanted. Imagine if all your thoughts were focused on all the reasons why you couldn't save money or borrow money. Imagine if all you thought about were the pathways that led you to failing to acquire the necessary funds you wanted. How different would the result have been?

This is an example of 'catastrophe thinking', having the mindset that everything is going to fail and believing the outcome you want will never happen. In its extreme, catastrophic thoughts lead to catastrophic outcomes. Fear is usually the cause of such thinking. But when the fear isn't there, especially the fear of failure, and you become more assured and less tentative, you start making better decisions. Better decisions lead to better outcomes. Better outcomes lead to greater success and fulfillment.

So it's quite pertinent to remember what Henry Ford said about the power of your thoughts and beliefs:

Whether you think you can, or think you can't, you're right.

You can choose what to think. You have that freedom. That is your power.

THE POWER OF EMOTION

Similarly, as with your thoughts, your emotions can either help you along the path to success or steer you down the path of failure. Your emotions can be the wind pushing your hot air balloon toward your destination, or they can be the anchor ropes tethering you to the spot. Or worse, the flames that burn your balloon to the ground and all your hopes and dreams with it.

Enthusiasm is a positive emotion that can drive you toward success. Not every enthusiastic person finds success, but like any fuel, people who achieve success have learned to use enthusiasm to propel them in the direction they want to go.

Enthusiasm stems from the Greek language meaning 'to be filled with God'. Enthusiasm flows from inspiration, which is to be 'in spirit'. It's the energy and excitement of doing something that you love doing. It's the emotion that drives you toward action, which is vital because without action you cannot succeed in your endeavours.

There are many inspiring emotions that can evoke your enthusiasm and power you to success. Such inspiring emotions include: the love of what you do, the bliss of creating, being in 'the flow', harmony with your environment, peace of mind, the joy of being alive, the freedom of unlimited being, the awareness of abundance, unconditional self-expression, and many more. The trick is to find the wave and catch it.

At beaches around the world, if surfers can find a wave that will give them a 15-second ride, that's a surfer's dream. That's heaven. Then they paddle back out again and catch the next one. Likewise, when I'm in the flow of writing it's as if I'm surfing a blissful wave. Only my wave can last *15 hours* at a time.

That's the power of emotion. It can be an endless source of energy, propelling you toward your goals. Yet, just as negative thoughts can derail the best of your plans, so too can negative emotions. To harbour and encourage emotions such as fear, anger, hate, greed, jealousy, resentment, spitefulness, superiority, is to harbour and encourage failure.

Why? Because these emotions are, for the most part, self-sabotaging emotions: they cause just as much damage internally as they do externally.

The Grimm's fairy tale of *Snow White and the Seven Dwarfs* is full of great lessons to not only children but also to adults, especially on the dangers of self-sabotaging emotions, particularly hatred.

In the fairy tale, the cruel queen, Snow White's stepmother, keeps Snow White enslaved and in rags, denying her royal rights as the daughter of the king. When the queen asks the magic mirror on the wall, "Who is the fairest of them all?" and hears that her stepdaughter, Snow White, is far lovelier and fairer than herself, the queen flies into a fit of rage and begins to plot her revenge. Her hatred and jealousy are all-consuming. Motivated by her twisted desires, she is even willing to commit murder to regain her title as the most beautiful and fairest in the land.

But the woodsman hired to do her dirty work doesn't have the heart to kill Snow White. Instead, he abandons her in the woods to fend for herself, but alive at least. Snow White survives with the help of forest animal friends—rabbits, squirrels, birds, deer—that lead her to the house of the seven dwarfs, where she finds shelter and rest.

She befriends the dwarfs and lives happily with them until the queen learns that she is still alive and sets out to kill her. Disguised as an old hag, the queen tracks Snow White to the dwarfs' house and offers her an apple, which Snow White can't resist. But the apple is poisoned with hatred and malice and evil, and, despite the warnings from her animal friends, Snow White takes a bite, whereupon she collapses.

Her animal friends seek out the dwarfs in the diamond mine in which they are working, urging them to return to the house to help Snow White, but it appears their efforts are in vain. Snow White is dead.

Then suddenly, a prince appears. He kisses her on the lips and brings her back to life. They return to the castle, the cruel queen is swept away in a ferocious storm, and Snow White and the prince live happily ever after. Like all good fairy tales, goodness triumphs over evil.

In her book, *Secret Door to Success*,[7] Florence Scovel Shinn explains the full symbolism of this fairy tale. The forest animals represent our hunches and intuitions, always working with our best intentions in mind and helping to get us 'out of the woods'. The seven dwarfs represent the positive forces of good, which aim to protect and serve us, to heal, to give shelter, to provide for. Snow White represents us, or more precisely, our innocent self, our unblemished self, our purest self.

---

[7] *Secret Door to Success*, Florence Scovel Shinn, DeVorss & Company, 1940

The cruel queen, Snow White's stepmother, represents our negative thought forms and emotions, either conscious or subconscious. These negative thought forms keep us enslaved and in rags, as all cruel and tyrannical thought forms and emotions do. They are poisonous and self-destructive. They care only for one thing, the ego's own existence and survival at any cost.

There are many more symbolic meanings throughout the fairy tale, such as the apple, the woodsman, the castle, and the prince. But we do not need to go deeper into them in this book other than to highlight that, like the queen, it is possible for your negative convictions and emotions to be swept away and drowned out so they no longer keep you enslaved and in rags. As long as you are vigilant to them and their self-destructive consequences. As long as you are aware of them and keep them within your sight.

Then you can free yourself from their control. That is your power.

THE POWER OF RESPONSE-ABILITY

Your instinctive, unconscious reactions and behaviours also play a significant role in determining your levels of success and happiness. How you react on impulse to people, events, ideas, and even yourself, can either set you on the path to success and freedom, or imprison you behind the bars of limitation and thoughtlessness.

Because success is a habit, successful people embrace the habit of being 'response-able'. This means they intentionally avoid reacting instinctively or without thought, and instead respond with poise and thoughtfulness. They make it a habit to take responsibility for how they think, feel, and act.

Unsuccessful people, however, tend to lack response-ability and usually act unthinkingly—they are habitually reactive, not proactive. They subcontract responsibility of their thoughts, emotions, and actions outside of themselves, thereby relinquishing control and putting themselves at the mercy of events, circumstances, and other people. This reluctance to accept response-ability is more akin to slavery than freedom.

Anatomically, a reflex is an action that bypasses the higher centres of the brain. For instance, you might have seen footage of a doctor tapping the knee of a patient with a patella hammer to check the patient's knee reflex, or you might have even had a doctor do it to you (see *Figure 3*). When the patella (kneecap) tendon is tapped, the muscle spindle in the quadriceps muscle (thigh) is stretched, which produces a chemoelectrical signal that travels via afferent sensory nerves up to the spinal cord at the level of L3 (Lumbar 3). At L3, the signal immediately rebounds to the quadriceps muscle via motor efferent nerves, triggering a contraction of the thigh and causing the foot to kick. This all happens independently of the brain.

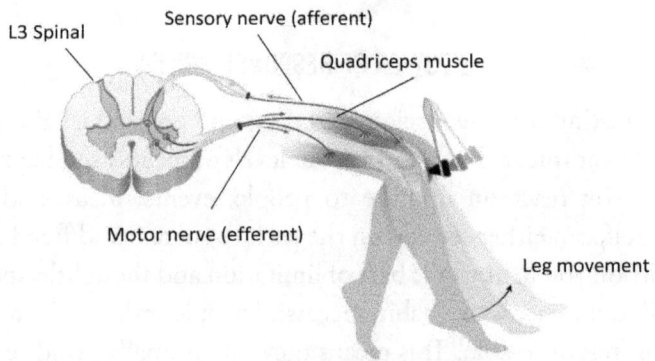

FIGURE 3: The Patella Reflex

Unfortunately, reflexes aren't just confined to the muscles of the body—our mind can react just as reflexively, and we can spend a great deal of our years in such an unthinking, reflexive state. What this means is that we can react to the sensory input of the world independently of our brains, and for many this can happen for the majority of our lives.

Thankfully, the problem isn't intrinsic and unchangeable. The problem, in fact, is inattention. The failure to be vigilant to what's happening, to have little or no focus on the here and now. When we are inattentive, we think, say, and do things that we are not conscious or aware of. Lack of awareness rarely leads to success. So our failures, more often than not, are the result of our failure to be vigilant and attentive.

Thankfully, you can always control your vigilance and focus. You can always control your attention, of being aware of your thoughts, your words, your behaviours. For instance, when you deliberately pilot your intentions to a specific destination or outcome, you are more likely to arrive at that destination or achieve that outcome. But if you lose focus and go into autopilot, you become habitually reactive and reflexive, thinking, saying, and doing things independently of your brain.

Reactive habits, however, are for the most part not productive or good habits. Reacting to others, to the world, to ourselves is not a good strategy for success. A better, more beneficial, strategy is to disengage your autopilot, engage your brain, and become *response-able*.

This is well within your control, and 'response-ability' works in this manner:

- -> When you are attentive of your thoughts, you are able to become more attentive of your emotions.
- -> When you are attentive of your emotions, you are able to become more attentive of your behaviour.
- -> And when you are attentive of your behaviour, you are able to respond with appropriate action—you are now response-*able*.

Only when you are response-able can you intentionally impact the way you want to live and who you want to be. If you don't, if you continue to be reflexive and reactive, you will remain where you are, unable to move forward, stuck in the same routine, unable to manifest the success you deserve.

Chuck M. Jones was the creator of Loony Tunes and all its wonderful characters—Bugs Bunny, Tweety Bird, Sylvester, Daffy Duck, Foghorn Leghorn, Marvin the Martian, Porky Pig, and many more. He once confessed that Bugs Bunny was the character that he always wished he was: suave, calm under pressure, laid back, always in control, everything always going right for him. In reality, he admitted, he was Daffy Duck; nothing seemed to go right, forever getting things wrong, tripping himself up all the time, everything falling apart at the seams. In essence, the cause of his own problems.

I think we can all relate to the Daffy Duck inside us at times. We can probably relate to the Bugs Bunny in others too, those who seem to always win, always get the rub of the green, nothing ever goes wrong for them, always able to pull themselves out of difficult situations without a scratch on them. They just seem to have it all.

But when you think about these two cartoon characters, you can see that Daffy Duck exhibits all the hallmarks of someone who is reactive and reflexive, and that Bugs Bunny is like someone who is non-reactionary and response-able. Daffy Duck reacts to external situations without thought; Bugs Bunny responds with poise and thoughtfulness.

Along those same lines, but on a more serious note, Viktor Frankl was a holocaust survivor who survived not one but two Nazi death camps during World War 2, after which he became the bestselling author of *Man's Search for Meaning*.[8] He was also a dual medical specialist in neurology and psychiatry, a remarkable feat in any time period. Yet, despite his horrifying experiences during

---

[8] *Man's Search for Meaning*, Viktor Frankl, Beacon Press, 1959 (first published 1946, Austria)

the war, he was still able to observe that no matter what happens to you, no matter what fate befalls you, you always have the free will to choose. He recognised that there was always a time gap between a cause and its effect. He called this time gap the 'space between stimulus and response'. Thus, he discovered, there was always a period of time between what's happening (stimulus) and your response to what's happening, no matter how short that time gap was.

Accordingly, you always have time to respond, you always have a 'space' in which you can choose how to act. In that space, Frankl said, is your power to choose your response, and in your response is your potential for growth and your freedom.

Putting this into context, in that time gap between stimulus and response is your power to be *response-able*. In your response-ability lies your growth and your freedom—your success.

That is your power.

2 THE RIGHT MINDSET

THE NO. 1 QUESTION

M. SCOTT PECK opened his famous book, *The Road Less Travelled*,[9] with the line, "Life is difficult."

This is along the same lines as Buddha, who said, "Everybody suffers," which simply means everybody is doing it hard, no matter who they are. That's everybody, every human being who has ever existed in the history of humanity. Nobody misses out. Which is why the Ancient Greek philosopher, Socrates, also advised that we should all be kind to each other, because everyone we meet is fighting a hard battle.

It's an age-old truism: Life is difficult. Everybody suffers, at least in some part of their life. You can't avoid it. Yet life is difficult for a number of reasons, and the reasons are different for different people. But there are some common difficulties we all face.

Self-doubt is certainly one of them. The doubt of not being good enough. The doubt of not knowing how to do what you want to do. The doubt of not being able to make the changes you need to improve your life. The doubt that nobody will accept who you are or care whether you're here or not.

Time, or the lack thereof, is another shared difficulty. Even though we live in a highly connected world, we seem to be incredibly time poor and overwhelmed by the everyday things we need to do to get by. Time is an ever-depleting commodity. We can never get more of it, no matter how hard we try.

---

[9] *The Road Less Travelled: A New Psychology of Love, Traditional Values and Spiritual Growth*, M. Scott Peck, Simon and Schuster, 1978

Then there's the cost of living—food, rent, mortgage, water, petrol, electricity, telephone, internet. Money, or the lack of it, is a very big problem for many people.

And we haven't even touched on relationships with family and friends, or even work, physical and mental health, education, emotional trauma, or social and sexual discrimination.

So, yes, life is difficult on many aspects. Life is challenging on many different levels. How, then, do you break free from your difficulties and reclaim your life for yourself?

By asking the right questions.

Einstein famously remarked that you can't solve your problems with the same thinking that created them. The same way of thinking is only going to result in the same outcomes. This is also true of the questions you ask. If you continually ask the same questions over and over again every single day, you will continually receive the same answers. So if the answers aren't working for you, you need to disrupt your previous thinking patterns. You need to ask different questions. Why? Because the secret to success reveals itself when you ask the right questions.

Where, though, would you begin?

How about at the very top? How about starting by asking the No. 1 question successful people ask?

And here it is. Here is the question that will go a long way to helping you break free from most, if not all, your difficulties:

What would a successful person in my position do?

Take a minute to reflect on this question. Is this something you've ever asked yourself? Have you ever considered what a successful person would do in your position? If not, it will be very much worth your while to ponder it.

The power behind this question is that it doesn't matter what you are currently doing. It doesn't matter who you are, where you are, when you are, or how you are. It doesn't matter what you've done in the past, the mistakes you've made, the regrets you have. All the question requires is for you to identify what a *successful person* would do given they face your current situation.

One of the first things a successful person would do to solve the difficulties they are facing, if not the very first thing, is to make sure they have the right mindset. They would get their mind right first. But what is the 'right' mindset?

To help you identify this, let's consider these four questions:

1. Would a successful person have a wholistic perspective?
2. Would a successful person invest their time wisely?
3. Would a successful person devote themselves to greater learning?
4. Would a successful person establish and grow their character and values?

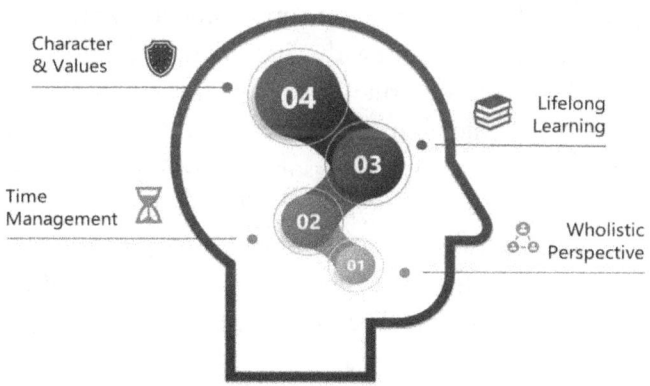

FIGURE 4:   The Right Mindset

Let's now discuss the things a successful person would be doing in your position.

#1: Would a successful person have a wholistic perspective?

There are many aspects to developing the right mindset, but one essential feature is perspective. They say that a pessimist sees the glass half-empty, and the optimist sees the glass half-full. But this isn't the end of the matter. There is another way of looking at the glass, and that's to step back and see that it is both.

For that's the truth, isn't it? The glass is at the same time both half-empty and half-full. It's only a matter of what you focus on that determines what you see, a glass half-empty or a glass half-full. Neither perspective is more correct than the other.

But it is more correct to say that the glass is both half-empty and half-full. The right mindset acknowledges this fact. It sees the whole. It acknowledges what is and accepts what is. It doesn't try to paint a pessimistic picture that the glass 'should' be fuller, or that there's something wrong with the glass because it is missing half its contents. It also doesn't try to paint an overly rosy picture of the glass and attempt to make it something other than what it is, fuller than half-full. The right mindset simply notices what is without judgement and goes to work with what's available.

In medicine, the doctrine of holism is the consideration of the patient as a 'whole' in the treatment of disease. That is, the healer considers the complete person—physically, physiologically, psychologically, and even psychically. The patient is viewed as a whole of her physical, mental, emotional, and spiritual parts with the understanding that each part can affect the health of another part. Every part is linked. For instance, mental health can affect physical health, spiritual health can affect emotional health, emotional health can affect mental health, and so forth. A holistic healer views the whole picture, not just the presenting symptoms and signs, and prescribes treatment based on this consideration of the whole.

We too can use this same doctrine in our everyday lives. We too can be 'wholistic'. We can see the 'whole' in everything that transpires throughout the day, taking note as things unfold just as they are without judgement. The glass is half-empty. The glass is half-full. But the practice of 'wholism' recognises and accepts that it is both. This is having the right mindset. Not pessimism, not optimism, but wholism.

The benefit of adopting this wholistic perspective is that you become more adaptable to changing circumstances, and adaptability is key to your growth and evolution. For example, instead of reacting negatively to a situation that is deemed 'bad' or detrimental (glass half-empty), you will respond constructively, trying to find the good that can come out of the current situation (glass half-full).

Let's consider the phenomenon of resistance. Resistance is a great example of dual perspective, whereby you can either use it constructively or use it detrimentally. Just as you can look at the glass half-full or half-empty, there is more than one angle to look at resistance. Some people interpret what's happening around them as negative, so they resist and oppose what is going on. This causes mental friction, which is felt as frustration, pain, and anger. Resistance becomes erosive, an abrasive force rubbing against them. Like sandpaper, life wears them down, but it's really their perspective that's wearing them down (and out).

But there is another perspective, one in which you can use resistance as an opportunity to expand and grow. Like weights at the gym, bodybuilders use resistance training to build muscle bulk and tone. They use resistance to build their strength and increase their stamina. They have learned to use opposing forces to their benefit. Airplanes use this same principle, as Henry Ford reminded us:

> *When everything seems to be going against you, remember that the airplane takes off against the wind.*

Taking off, then, is just looking at life's difficulties with the right perspective and positioning yourself at the right angle. With correct perspective, you will make the most of what's available given the current situation. You won't moan and complain that there's nothing to work with, that things would be a whole lot better if the circumstances were different. You will develop a 'can do' attitude. You won't harbour 101 reasons why things can't get done. You will see the direction of the wind, then ask how you can use what you have to take off. With this perspective, you will use each moment to work for you, not against you. Each moment will become an opportunity for healing and growth, not a problem to be shunned and avoided.

This 'can do' attitude will more likely than not lead you up the higher road of resourcefulness and belief. The danger of a 'can't do' attitude, however, is that it will eventually lead you down the road of cynicism and doubt. There's simply no other route it can take. One road leads to success, the other road leads to failure.

As an infant, Helen Keller (1880-1968) suffered a debilitating illness that left her deaf, blind, and mute. Yet despite living in a world deprived of vision and hearing, Keller transcended her disabilities and became a bestselling author and international speaker. She helped found the American Civil Liberties Union and was awarded the Presidential Medal of Freedom. She even graduated magna cum laude from Radcliffe in 1904.

Throughout her life, Keller wrote and spoke about happiness and living with purpose and meaning. Through all her tribulations, she came to the realisation that life, even with all its dangers and fears, was either a daring adventure or it was nothing at all. She had discovered that to live a life to the fullest, you need the right attitude and mindset. When you come to the fork in the road, you need to decide which one will take you higher, not take you down. She said:

THE RIGHT MINDSET

Be of good cheer. Do not think of today's failures, but of the success that may come tomorrow... We can do anything we want to if we stick to it long enough.

If somebody who couldn't see, couldn't hear, and couldn't speak was able to establish the right mindset and achieve the success and happiness that most people dream about, where does that leave us who are more fully abled? What excuses do we have not to find that 'can do' attitude that will propel us to our greatest achievements, to dare us to live with enthusiasm and adventure, to lift us to our own success and happiness?

'CAN DO' ATTITUDE	'CAN'T DO' ATTITUDE
Sees what can be done.	Sees roadblocks and obstacles.
Focuses on what they want.	Focuses on what they don't want.
Seeks to be response-able.	Seeks to hide from responsibility.
Embraces difficulties and challenges.	Avoids difficulties and hard work.
Thinks of reasons why it can happen.	Has 101 excuses why it can't happen.
Believes things will work out well.	Believes things will end badly.
Abundance and adventure mindset.	Paucity and danger mindset.
Motto: 'Life, teach me what I need to learn.'	Motto: 'Life, give me what I want.'

TABLE 1:   Can Do Vs Can't Do Attitude

If you have a 'can't do' mindset, you will allow the doubts to keep piling up and prevent you from doing what you need to do. As a Doubting Thomas, you will waste time and procrastinate. You will focus on self-limiting beliefs and fears that reinforce the notion that you aren't good enough. You won't believe 'somebody like me' can be successful.

A Doubting Thomas will never finish, let alone start, their journey to success. But as someone with a 'can do' mindset, you won't allow doubts and fears to dominate your thinking. You won't allow doubts or fears to dictate how you behave or affect your belief in yourself or your abilities.

Sure, every successful person has doubts and faces fear. They are human. But they don't allow the doubts and fears to run amok and derail them from achieving their goal. They are like teachers, getting a class of rowdy kids to stand quietly in line and behave. The doubts and fears are there, but they are controlled and kept in line.

You can also do this. That's your power.

#2: *Would a successful person invest their time wisely?*

As well has developing a wholistic perspective, having the right mindset also means to be disciplined in managing your time. Your mind and your time are your most valuable assets. Your imagination, how you think, is your most valuable inner asset, and how you spend or invest your time is your most valuable external asset.

> *To be effective and successful, you will need to utilise your mind and your time to your maximum capability.*

Time is the medium from which money flows and grows, not the other way around: time does not flow from money, and no matter how much money you have you cannot buy yourself more time. This is why time is more valuable than money. Time is a

THE RIGHT MINDSET

diminishing asset, which makes it extraordinarily valuable. You can always bank more money, but you can never bank more time. So you'd do well to be mindful of the phrase:

Don't save money by spending time.

But whereas most people see the benefits of having a household or business budget, many do not implement the same care or accountability with their time. They budget their income and expenditure, but they don't budget their time. Instead, they waste time, or they 'kill' time.

This is not how successful people utilise their time. They are good time managers. They don't waste time or kill time, instead they find ways to free more time for themselves and for the things they want to do and achieve.

Likewise, if your intent is to increase your effectiveness and achieve special goals, good time-management is essential. Yet, the best time-managers are also the best self-managers. The passage of time is beyond your control, because irrespective of anything you do, time keeps flowing. What you can control, however, is how you manage yourself in the time that you have.

What this means is that good time-management is good self-management. The investment of time is the investment of self. The value of time is the value of self.

Conversely, if you don't value your time, you are in effect admitting that you don't value yourself. Members of The 5% Club value themselves. They invest their time wisely because they know it is an investment in self. They invest time by allocating time every week for their goals and are extremely protective of it. That means no interruptions—no phone calls, no visitors, no meetings, no emails, no distractions at all—because they know how valuable their time is and nothing is going to take it away from them.

A great time-management (and self-management) technique is to ask: *Where does my time go now?*

This is best achieved through a two-step process:

1. Time Audit:[10] To find out where you are spending your time now, a good idea is to keep a time log for 2-4 days. Write down in half-hour blocks what you have been doing over the past 24-hours. The results will surprise you.
2. Identify Time Thieves: The second thing to do is to eliminate time-stealers and time-wasters. The best way to do this is to make a list of your time-stealers and time-wasters at home and at work. The time audit will help you immensely with this. Then write down one time-waster that you are committed to eliminating in your life in the next week, and how you will achieve this.

The greatest investment you can ever make is your time because the dividends and return of such investment is multiplied within yourself. That's your power.

#3: Would a successful person devote themselves to greater learning?

The right mindset also means the attitude of wanting to be better today than you were yesterday, and to be better tomorrow than you are today. To aim for the highest goal, to be a master of your craft. To want to be known as an expert in your field. To want to be known for knowing something.

To know something is to be knowledgeable, and knowledge, as they say, is power. Knowledge is the minimum requirement for entry into The 5% Club, but not the kind of knowledge you might be thinking. You don't need the knowledge that is learned from universities or other higher education centres. Professors,

---

[10] Readers can download a 24-hour Time Audit PDF by visiting my website at www.scottzarcinas.com/time-audit

THE RIGHT MINDSET

PhD graduates, post-graduates, and even multiple degree holders aren't necessarily given automatic entry into The 5% Club. A lot of members are high school or university dropouts. They are self-made, having learned from the hardest school of all, the School of Hard Knocks. Yet, you don't even need the knowledge of experience or adversity to be given admission.

The kind of knowledge you need is self-knowledge. This is the kind of knowledge the Ancient Greeks valued above all else: to Know Thy Self. As we know, self-knowledge is inner power, the only power that counts—the power to choose, the power to make and shape your moments.

The opposite of knowledge is ignorance. Where knowledge empowers, ignorance disempowers. Where self-knowledge is self-empowering, ignorance saps your power. Like the Ancient Greeks, members of The 5% Club cherish self-knowledge above all other knowledge. They understand intuitively that curiosity didn't kill the cat, ignorance did. Especially ignorance of self. Be curious, then, and keep what the Buddhists call 'Beginner's mind'.[11]

> *If your mind is empty, it is open to everything. In the beginner's mind there are many possibilities, but in the expert's mind there are few.*

In the beginning of any new venture, such as learning a new language, starting a new career, picking up a musical instrument, you probably won't know very much about this new thing you are learning. You certainly won't be proficient for quite some while in French, or Spanish, or Chinese, or whatever new language you are starting to learn. You won't start out as a CEO or director of the new company you've just started, more likely you'll be assigned a more junior role. You won't be an immediate maestro of your new instrument either, just a student learning where to place your hands to clunk the keyboard or pluck the strings.

[11] *Zen Mind, Beginner's Mind*, Shunryu Suzuki, Weatherhill, 1970

As a beginner, you won't start out as a favoured translator for the United Nations, nor will you be Steve Jobs or Jack Welch. Nor will you be Elton John or Jimmie Hendricks. You will very much be a beginner, and that's a great and exciting place to be because you'll have a beginner's mindset and your learning curve will be huge. When you have beginner's mind, you are open to explore all possibilities. You are vigilant for ways to improve yourself and your skillsets. You are accepting of your mistakes and errors.

Then, after a while, after you've learned the new skills and have become more proficient in your new endeavour, you begin to lose the beginner's mindset. The ego kicks in and you're not so open to explore all possibilities anymore, maybe even dismissive of new ideas, because you now assume you've learned the best way to do it. You no longer seek ways to improve yourself or your skillsets because you assume you've reached the pinnacle. You are less accepting of your mistakes and errors, and those of others, because you've adorned the mantle of an expert, and experts can't be seen to make mistakes.

The trap to avoid is to believe you know it all. This is narrow-minded thinking and it closes you off to further learning and opportunities. No matter how advanced you've become, the trick to maintaining the openness of a beginner's mind is to approach every situation as if it's the first time you've seen it. Beginner's mind is the mindset of growth and success, and one way to keep hold of beginner's mind is to always be curious.

When you are confronted with challenges or obstacles, you might find yourself resisting the situation or being overwhelmed with the problems at hand. You might evaluate the problem as being too hard, or that your solution to it won't work. You might also think the solution is too expensive, that it isn't worth the effort or the time you need to invest to solve the problem. You might even throw your hands in the air and complain that everything you've tried has come to no avail.

But to think like this is to close your beginner's mind and rob yourself of the opportunity to grow and succeed. Instead of assuming, 'This won't work,' rather be curious and ask yourself, 'How will this work?' Instead of thinking the cost in money or time or effort is too high, rather be curious and ask yourself, 'How will I pay for this?' Instead of complaining that everything you've tried has failed to result in a positive outcome, rather be curious and ask yourself, 'How can I turn defeat into victory?'

Be curious then. Curiosity will keep your beginner's mind open. Curiosity will keep you fresh, keep you young. Be curious of everything. Also be just as curious of your inner world as you are of your outer world. Those who are always curious always learn and grow; and those who always learn and grow are successful in what they set out to achieve.

Here are some of the benefits of being curious:

INNER KNOWLEDGE	OUTER KNOWLEDGE
Joy of life and deep happiness.	Joy of discovery and learning.
Energised and invigorated.	Keeping fresh (not stale, not bored).
Inner manifestation of peace.	Outer manifestatin of intentions.
Self-love and self-acceptance.	Patience and non-judgement.
Improved relationship with self.	Improved relationships with others.
Inner growth and freedom.	External success and achievement.
Calm and relaxation.	In the flow / in the zone.
Oneness and abundance.	Connectedness and empathy.

TABLE 2:   Benefits of Being Curious

Jeff Bezos, the founder of Amazon, one of the most successful companies on the planet, embraced this philosophy from the very beginnings of Amazon in the 1990s as an online seller of books. When asked to divulge the secret of his success, Bezos ascribed the incredible rise of Amazon to innovation. Amazon, to Bezos, was always an innovative business. It keeps learning. It keeps researching. It keeps inventing. It never rests on its laurels, always assuming that it can always improve, always be better.

Likewise, you need to be innovative if you want to succeed. You do this by continuing to be curious, to keep learning, to keep getting better, to reach the point of mastery. Aim to become a master of what you do. More importantly, aim to become a master of your inner world. A master never stops learning. A master is a perpetual student of life and is dedicated to a lifelong learning of her craft, and a lifelong learning of herself.

Mastery of self is well within your reach. That's your power.

#4: Would a successful person establish and grow their character and values?

The right mindset also utilises the second tenet of success, to be fully aware that success comes through you, not to you. To know through direct experience that who you are being is more important than what you are doing. To understand what the 19th Century British philosopher, James Allen, said about the power of being in his classic book, *As a Man Thinketh*:[12]

> *Men do not attract that which they want, but that which they are.*

Character and values are the foundation of who you are, and they are therefore the foundation of any success you wish to achieve. Your character is the embodiment and personification of

---

[12] *As a Man Thinketh*, James Allen, D. MacKay Company, 1890

your inner values. A person of great character is dedicated to great values. A person of great value holds great values.

Some character traits and values that successful people adhere to are:

-> Courage and bravery—to do what's right despite the fear.

-> Honesty and integrity—to always be true to yourself, to your dreams, and to others.

-> Resilience and persistence—to never give up, to always move forward despite the odds against you.

-> Compassion and kindness—to value kindness over aggression, caring over apathy.

-> Respect and acceptance—to respect other people and accept other opinions as valid and important.

-> Gratitude and thanksgiving—to be grateful for all that you have and to give thanks for the lessons others show you.

-> Giving and service—to give unto others that which you wish for yourself, and to be of value through service to others.

These are just some of the character traits and values you can incorporate into your identity, who you are and want to be, knowing that the level of your success will depend on the level of your commitment to them. To put these character traits into perspective, consider their opposite traits and the effect they would have on your attitude, emotions, and actions, and thus your level of success:

-> Cowardice and timidity—running away from your responsibilities and failing to stand up for what's right.

-> Dishonesty and deceit—failing to be true to yourself, ignoring your dreams, and cheating others.

-> Resignation and apathy—to never give anything a try, to stay stuck and refuse to progress.

-> Cruelty and maliciousness—to be quick to anger, to resort to violence, to bully others.

-> Disrespect and dismissiveness—to disrespect other people and reject other opinions as invalid and unimportant.

-> Ingratitude and ungraciousness—to be ungrateful for what you have, to take everything and everyone for granted, to be self-entitled.

-> Greedy and covetous—to take from others that which you wish for yourself, to be totally selfish, and to be of no value whatsoever to others.

You can now see why success comes to those who establish and grow their character.

THE NEXT QUESTION

We've now asked a lot of questions, but there's probably one more question we should add to the list:

What would be the real cost of not developing the right mindset?

What would the cost be of not having a wholistic perspective, of allowing a 'can't do' attitude to take control of your thoughts, emotions, and behaviours?

What would the cost be of not being a good time manager, to be ill-disciplined and fail to protect your most valuable external asset—time?

THE RIGHT MINDSET

What would the cost be of not being curious, of not dedicating yourself to lifelong learning, of not becoming a master of your craft?

What would the cost be of thinking that your strength of character and values are of no importance to who you are and what you identify with?

When you deeply realise the enormous cost of not having the right mindset, you will fast track yourself into doing everything in your power to develop it. The cost of lost happiness, lost love, lost peace, lost time, lost money, lost wisdom, lost harmony, lost effectiveness, lost relationships. The cost simply isn't worth it.

It is difficult, sure. Life is difficult. We all know that. The next question therefore is not, "What will I do to be as success?" but:

What will I ask to be a success?

3 IMAGINATION, INTENTION & ATTITUDE

THE 3 CORE ATTRIBUTES OF POWERFUL HABITS

FUNDAMENTAL TO DEVELOPING the right mindset is the correct utilisation of the power of your thoughts, emotions, and instinctive behaviours. To be aware that your thoughts, emotions, and instincts can either work for you or work against you. To know that your success in the Game of Life is dependent on how you think, feel, and behave.

Here is what every member of The 5% Club knows and what 95% of the world doesn't know:

> *When you purposefully direct the power of your thoughts, emotions, and behaviours to your desired outcomes, you awaken a slumbering force that can move mountains.*

Be, therefore, deliberately thoughtful. Be emotionally centred. Be response-able. Then follow the process that everyone in The 5% Club follows, which is none other than the strategy of success we've been discussing: Identity, Purpose, Conviction.

- -> *Identity*: Create a vision of who you want to be and what you want to achieve.
- -> *Purpose*: Spark your enthusiasm and determination through desire and will.
- -> *Conviction*: Formulate a plan, be disciplined in sticking to that plan, and build habits that will keep you following that plan toward your goals.

Then repeat this process over and over again until you manifest your success. But don't expect to magically achieve your goals at the click of your fingers. Overnight success takes 20 years to develop, as they say. Rather, do as Arnold Schwarzenegger advised: create a vision of who you want to be and what you want to achieve, then grow into that vision as if it were already there.

Remember, success takes time. You will therefore need to make Identity, Purpose, and Conviction a habit. These are not things you can just set and forget. You will need to commit to them and tend to them regularly. This means work, hard work. You will need to work hard on your identity, creating a vision of your ideal self, your ideal life. You will need to work hard on staying focused and undistracted on your purpose, keeping your strength of will. You will need to work hard on maintaining your discipline and conviction, staying the course when others have given up.

To develop and amplify the components of Identity, Purpose, and Conviction, and get the most out of life, there are 3 Core Attributes you need to activate. These attributes you already have. You don't have to look for them, they are already part of you. Then all you do is hone them every day like a samurai warrior hones his sword. These 3 Core Attributes are:

1. Imagination.
2. Intention.
3. Attitude.

They are like three slumbering superpowers. You already have Imagination. You already have Intention. You already have Attitude. You just need to awaken them.

Once your superpowers are awakened, you are then able to develop and amplify the three components of success we've been discussing:

IMAGINATION, INTENTION & ATTITUDE

1. Identity—'I Am!'
2. Purpose—'I Will!'
3. Conviction—'I Can!'

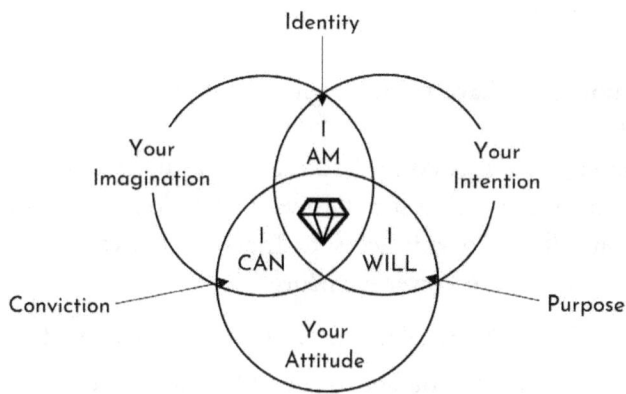

FIGURE 5:   The 3 Core Attributes of Powerful Habits

I Am! I Will! I Can! are developed through Imagination, Intention, and Attitude in this way:

-> The overlap where your Imagination and Intention align is where you get clarity of who you are and what you want to become by defining your *identity*—your 'I Am'.

-> Next, the overlap where your Intention and Attitude align is where you build your motivation and drive by determining your *purpose* and cause— your 'I Will'.

-> Finally, the overlap where your Attitude and Imagination align is where you solidify your *conviction* and self-belief by designing the pathway to your destination—your 'I Can'.

But where your real riches are to be found is the central overlap where the three components of 'I Am', 'I Will', and 'I Can' merge and align as one Power Source. This is where you will find your fortune and success. Not outside you, but inside you.

Our aim, therefore, is to tap into this Power Source as often as we can. The more often we tap into it, the longer we are 'switched on', the more power we have to make and shape our moments, the more power we have to live a life of fulfillment, happiness, and abundance.

Tapping into this Power Source, which can be difficult, is like unlocking a safe with a secret code. This code is a kind of secret PIN you will need to gain access to The 5% Club, and it is based on four principles, or 4 Power Elements:

1. *Faith*: the belief in who you are and what you do.
2. *Valour*: the courage to live a life that's authentic and true to who you are.
3. *Value*: the value you bring to others and to the world around you.
4. *Commitment*: the investment of yourself into everything you do.

Each Power Element is the culmination of its corresponding Power Habit:

-> Power Habit #1: Self-Assuredness & Self-Belief produces the Power Element of *Faith*.

-> Power Habit #2: Courage & Confidence produces the Power Element of *Valour*.

-> Power Habit #3: Other People Thinking produces the Power Element of *Value*.

-> Power Habit #4: Planning, Preparation & Perseverance produces the Power Element of *Commitment*.

IMAGINATION, INTENTION & ATTITUDE

As each Power Habit is developed through your Imagination, Intention, and Attitude, access to this secret code and the unlocking of your fortune and success all starts with the awakening of your superpowers, so let's now discuss these in more detail.

AWAKENING YOUR IMAGINATION SUPERPOWER

It's interesting that society puts so much emphasis on knowledge. We worship our knowledge not too unlike our ancestors worshipped the sun and the moon. We value expertise. We pay a premium for those who have specialised knowledge and skills, like lawyers, doctors, business consultants, financial advisers, engineers, rocket scientists, and the like.

But Einstein didn't. He valued imagination far more than knowledge. He valued the human brain's capacity to think far more than the brain's capacity to store and retrieve knowledge. He said:

Imagination is more important than knowledge.
Knowledge has limits.

Not that knowledge isn't important. Of course it is. The quest for knowledge and truth is noble and essential for the growth and evolution of humankind.

Knowledge, we know, is power. Yet, as Einstein observed, human knowledge is limited. Human imagination has no limits, which makes it infinitely more powerful. If knowledge is a train progressing along the tracks and picking up passengers along the way, imagination is the Starship *Enterprise*, free to boldly go where no-one has gone before.

Only with imagination can we reach the stars.

As an author, I'm often invited to attend school assemblies and ceremonies as a guest speaker. On one such occasion, I was asked to be the guest of honour at a book giving ceremony at a primary school in an under-developed part of the city, and to give a short speech.

Seated on the stage, I waited for the children to enter the hall and sit on the floor in front of me. The first thing that struck me was the vast diversity of the children: kids seemingly from all over the world; Africa, Asia, Indigenous, Sub-continent, Middle-East, Europe. There were also, it seemed, a higher-than-normal percentage of physically and intellectually disabled children.

Looking at this diverse bunch of underprivileged, yet eager and smiling kids, I folded my prepared speech and shoved it in my back pocket, deciding instead to give another entirely different presentation. Although it had been fermenting in my mind for some while, this would be the first time I had given this particular speech. I figured these kids would be the best critics to test the waters, and if it went down well with them, I was certain I'd be able to deliver it to any crowd.

Summarising the talk, I first reminded them that each and every one of them had a superpower. Because they were unique, because they were human, because they were the only human being in the entire history of humankind to exist just as them, they had a superpower they could use at any time of day or night. They had a superpower they could count on to use whenever they needed it. A superpower that was on-demand and limitless.

This superpower was their *imagination*.

This superpower could be used in any way they wanted. It could be used to invent new things to help them, their families, their community, the human race. Edison had used his imagination to invent the movie camera and improve the electric light bulb. Somebody, somewhere in the distant past had invented the wheel. Tim Berners-Lee had invented the world wide web.

IMAGINATION, INTENTION & ATTITUDE

What could they invent?

Imagination, I went on, could also be used to create and build things that had never been seen before. J.K. Rowling created the world of Harry Potter. Da Vinci created the Mona Lisa. Jørn Utzon created the Sydney Opera House.

What could they create?

It didn't stop there, either. Imagination could also be used to improve on things that already existed, things that are good now but could be even better. Enzo Ferrari saw what mechanics had done with the motor car in the 1950s and took his flashing red machine to the next level. Steve Jobs saw the lumpy, heavy computers of the 70s and early 80s and imagined a world in which you could buy a computer in a gift box. Coco Chanel reimagined the fashion industry, and her label became synonymous with luxury and haute couture.

What could they improve upon? What could they imagine?

What, in fact, can you imagine?

A World of Possibility

The message I wanted to give these kids is the same message I want to give you now:

> *Imagination opens your eyes to the opportunities that surround you.*

Imagination gives your eye focus, your mind clarity. Like Superman's x-ray vision, it enables you to see what has previously remained hidden, which is a superpower. This why Einstein valued imagination so much, and why he also said:

> *Imagination is everything. It is the preview of life's coming attractions.*

We need our imagination superpower to see clearly, to see far, to see over the horizon. We also need imagination to inspire us. When we use our imagination, we are transported to another world of possibilities, another universe of what can be. We can then take that vision of what we've seen and bring it into the world in which we live, energised with the belief that it can be done, that we can help make this world a better place for ourselves, our children, and future generations.

Consider what our world could be if we all used our imagination to our greatest capacity.

Yet it's been estimated by psychologists and neuroscientists that human beings, on average, use less than 10% of their brain's capacity. Some say even less, barely 5-6%.

How, then, can we maximise our superpower? How can we make the most of our unique human brain? How can we fire up our imagination?

It's a question I don't even need to ask kids. They use their imagination all the time. They're masters at it. But something happens during our school years to snuff it out, and by the time we've entered adult life, our superpowers have been forgotten and our imagination barely used at all. Usually because we're told to stop daydreaming in class. So we do.

Thankfully, your superpower can be awakened from its slumber and revived from its dormancy. All you need do is this:

1. Acknowledge you have a superpower called Imagination—you can only use what you believe you have.
2. Spend a minimum of 30 minutes a day (1 hour is better) dedicated to using your Imagination superpower—like a muscle, you need to use it to build strength and prevent it from atrophying.

IMAGINATION, INTENTION & ATTITUDE

3. Don't judge, fear, or doubt your ideas—your Imagination thrives on being limitless and free; judgement, scorn, ridicule, doubt, and fear are like kryptonite to your imagination superpower. Treat each idea that you are working on as something that needs only to be accepted and nurtured to grow into its full potential. Then see where it takes you.
4. Test and persist—the best ideas are tested in the School of Life. Do the experiment and see where it goes. A sure way for an idea to die is to leave it to fade away in your mind. Also persist with it; an idea will probably not be the finished article and may not work the first time, but with polishing and persistence it will shine.
5. Have fun—the joy of using your Imagination superpower is eternal. Use it to release the fun, excitement, and enthusiasm of life that may also be dormant in your adult body but was ever-present when you were a child.

Children know that everybody has a superpower. Do you use yours?

AWAKENING YOUR INTENTION SUPERPOWER

Sometimes it can feel as if you are caught in a never-ending battle with life. The constant battles are wearying. Health battles. Money battles. Relationship battles. Work battles. Emotional battles. Food battles. Traffic battles. There are so many battles on so many fronts that at the end of every day you can feel like a soldier returning from the frontline of war. Warn out. Exhausted. Weary.

Weariness, though, isn't just confined to individuals. Families can feel it. Communities can feel it. Even nations can feel it, and the exhaustion and low spirits that a nation feels when subjected to a long period of fighting is known as 'war weariness'. When a nation is weary, there is simply no appetite for the prolongation of conflict or war. The price for fighting that conflict has become too high. The financial burden becomes too great. Civilian and military casualties mount up. Losses far outweigh the potential gains for continuing the fight. Weariness sets in.

It happened to the British when under siege from Nazi forces in World War 2, and it took a master leader, Winston Churchill, to see the fight through to victory despite the weariness of his nation. It also happened to the Germans toward the end of the war, when the Allied bombings flattened their cities night after night and their troops were forced into retreat across all fronts. It took the liberation of the German people from their own Nazi government to steer the country back toward democratic freedom and economic prosperity.

In both the UK and Germany, it was the collective strength of will that got them through. The will of the British people got them through their darkest hour, and the will of the German people galvanised them to rebuild their country. Both countries discovered the power of collective intention and exploited it to their advantage.

On an individual level, you too can exploit the power of intention to your advantage. You too can use the power of your will to get through your darkest hours, to overcome weariness, and to triumph over the odds.

But to do this you need to get your mindset right. Weak intention will not go the distance. Weak intention will crumble at the first challenge. So you need to activate and strengthen your intention. You need a strong will that will carry you through your weariness to that endpoint you want to arrive at. You need a strong will that can prepare you for the long haul and face the challenges you will meet. You need Churchillian resilience, of never giving up no matter the battle ahead.

IMAGINATION, INTENTION & ATTITUDE

Like Imagination, your Intention has superpower-like qualities. You just need to awaken and hone it. One of the best ways to activate your Intention is to give yourself a regular 'PEP talk'. The process to follow is this:

> P: Activate Your *Passion*—engage your inner drive and fully immerse yourself in it.
> E: Activate Your *Energy-Management Systems*— identify your energy drains and release your second wind.
> P: Activate *Project You*—build an air castle that the outside world cannot wreck.

Let's discuss these points in more detail.

P: Activate Your Passion

There are two main drivers that successful people align themselves with and identify as: the passion-driven, and the project-minded—swimmers and snipers, respectively. We will talk about snipers in a moment, but first we'll talk about swimmers.

Swimmers are passion-driven. They swim in the ocean of their passion and immerse themselves in the act of creation for as long as they can keep their eyes open. They dive into their passion, swimming with the undercurrents of their imagination, and only awakening after many hours with the feeling that only seconds have passed. They are caught in the 'flow of life', and if they're really good, they learn to surf on the waves of bliss for years on end.

Swimmers are generally, but not always, creative thinkers. They are right-brain dreamers and visionaries. They are masters of their Imagination superpower, and they use it to create the world and the environment in which they want to live.

Swimmers see things as they could be and as they want them to be.

Swimmers have usually known what they were going to do with their life from a very early age. They knew they were born for a certain task, and it wasn't going to be any other way. In fact, it was as impossible for them to be or do anything else as it was for them to change their DNA. It's simply who they are and what they do.

Ex-Formula 1 driver, Michael Schumacher, is an example of a swimmer. After winning his 7th Formula 1 world title and at the peak of his career, a racetrack reporter asked him how it felt to create history in his sport.

He replied, "I was born to race motorcars."

He knew in every cell of his body that he was born to fulfill this role. He committed and dedicated his entire being to racing, his chosen career. There was simply nothing else he was going to be or do. He had found his passion, which had led him to his life-purpose.

When Schumacher looked into the TV camera and spoke those words, it was as if he was talking directly to me. When I heard him speak of being born to race motorcars, I knew exactly how he felt. I too knew what I was born to be, a writer. I felt it from an early age (and still do) with every cell of my body. It's where I dive into my passion and find my bliss.

Like Schumacher, like all swimmers, the key is getting in 'the flow state'. The flow state is the term coined by psychologist Mihaly Czikszentmihalyi. Some call it 'the zone', but it's essentially the same thing—the state of intense absorption where you forget yourself and your surroundings, especially when you are doing something creative.

So a great way to activate your Intention superpower is to dive into your passion and fully immerse yourself in it. You can do this by asking yourself these questions:

- ♦ "What's my passion?"
- ♦ "Am I a swimmer or a sniper?"

IMAGINATION, INTENTION & ATTITUDE

- "Where do I find my bliss?"
- "What is the one thing that I am willing to sacrifice everything for?"
- "When was the last time I was in 'the flow', and what was I doing at the time?"
- "What did I do as a kid when I was so absorbed in what I was doing that I'd lose all track of time?"

The answer to these questions will activate your passion.

E: Activate Your Energy-Management Systems

There are many things that can cause you to feel disempowered—limited finances, lack of employment, relationship breakdown, severe illness, disabling injury, lack of education.

Yet one of the things that can work in your favour and empower you, no matter your circumstances, is having a clear vision of who you are, what you want to do, why you do it, and how to do it.

> *When you have clarity, you tap into the unlimited source of energy and enthusiasm at the core of your being.*

Like happiness, this energy and enthusiasm is always available, as long as you tap into it. Music is analogous to this unlimited source of energy. Or rather, the silence behind the music is analogous to this unlimited source of energy.

Consider a chamber orchestra at a concert and each note that is drifting to your ears. Music flows from note to note at different tempos and dynamics, but between each note is a period of silence. The music you are hearing is therefore the presence and the absence of consecutive notes. Without the notes there is no music, but without the silence separating the notes there is no music either, just continuous noise. So music flows in a procession of note to silence to note to silence to note to silence.

But at a deeper level of understanding, there is only silence; a musical note is just the vibration of the silence from which it emanates. But how, you may ask, can silence make a noise? Think of the mirror-like surface of a still lake at dawn. When a rock is dropped into the lake, ripples are created. Prior to the ripples there was only stillness. The rock has injected an energy force into the surface of the lake, creating wave forms, or ripples. Then, when the energy dissipates, the ripples fade away and stillness returns to the lake surface.

Likewise, when primal silence vibrates, a note is expressed, a waveform, a ripple. Then, when the silence stops vibrating, the notes fade away and nothing is heard, just the absence of a note, the original, primal silence. But the notes do not exist because of the absence of sound, music notes *emerge from* the silence just as ripples emerge from the stillness of the lake surface. In the same way, your thoughts emerge from the silent stillness of your mind. Just as the lake surface is the source of all ripples and waveforms, your mind is the source of all your thoughts. Your thoughts do not create your mind. They cannot do this any more than ripples can create the lake on which they exist.

Your mind is the progenitor, your thoughts are its progeny.

To use another analogy, fish swimming in the sea. Fish come and go, but the sea remains. So too music notes swim in the infinite ocean of silent no-sound. Music notes come and go, but the silence remains. The silence creates the music, not the other way around. Likewise, your mind is the ocean in which your thoughts arise and swim

We are delving into deep concepts here, but stick with me because it will all make sense in just a minute.

Let's extrapolate this concept of 'Primal Silence' to time, matter, and space. Each second of time is created from the eternal now. Each thing is created from the absolute no-thing. Each cubic

IMAGINATION, INTENTION & ATTITUDE

nanometre of space is created from the infinite emptiness.[13] We know this from Einstein's equation: $E = MC^2$. Where E is energy, M is mass, and C is the speed of light. At the most fundamental level of life, everything is energy. Energy is mass, and mass is energy. Time is energy, and energy is time. Space is energy, and energy is space. Everything you can feel, smell, see, taste, and hear are just different forms of the same universal energy field that created it. Same energy, different feel. Same energy, different thoughts. Same energy, different notes.

When the universal energy field vibrates, tiny sub-atomic particles come into being, just like music. These sub-atomic particles clump together to create atomic particles, like protons, neutrons, and electrons. Atomic particles clump together to create ions. Ions clump together to create molecules. Molecules clump to create chemical compounds. Chemical compounds clump together to form inorganic matter and organic matter. Matter forms every non-living and every living thing you see.

But everything comes from energy and is sustained by energy. This is the same universal energy field that you come from, the same energy field which sustains you.

> *Like music notes swimming in the ocean of silence, like fish swimming in the sea, like thoughts swimming in the stillness of your mind, everyone and everything is swimming in the universal field of energy from which the entire universe is created.*

Max Planck (1858-1957) is considered the father of quantum physics and was awarded the Nobel prize in 1918 for physics for his work on the establishment and development of the theory of elementary quanta. He spoke of the 'matrix of all matter' as an underlying force or consciousness giving rise to all matter. In

---

[13] This is the basis of the Big Bang Theory, which postulates that the universe exploded out of nothingness.

1936, in his address on the 25th anniversary of the formation of the Kaiser-Wilhelm Gesellschaft (Society), he said:

> *My research on the atom has shown me that there is no such thing as matter in itself. What we perceive as matter is merely the manifestation of a force that causes the subatomic particles to oscillate and holds them together in the tiniest solar system of the universe.*

This includes you. You are energy. You are an energy being. Your body is energy. Your thoughts are energy. Your emotions are energy. Your body, thoughts, and emotions are just different forms of the underlying energy field from which you arise. These forms manifest and present to your awareness in different ways, but they all stem from the same source, which is energy.

This is where it gets interesting. It may surprise you that you can control this flow of energy and how it manifests. You have this power, and the way you control this flow of energy is through *intention*. Your mind, or conscious awareness, is the means by which you can determine how this energy flows within you, and even outside of you. Like a dimmer switch dials up or dials down the electrical current to your bedroom light, your intentions dial up or dial down the energy current to your body, thoughts, and emotions.

Dial up your energy and you feel lighter. Your body feels more energetic and powerful, your thoughts are more positive and empowering, your emotions are more enthusiastic and exciting. This is your natural state of being, and it feels inspired, joyous, peaceful, and free. Dial down your energy, however, and you feel heavier. Your body feels lethargic and weak, your thoughts are negative and disempowering, and your emotions are apathetic and dispirited. This is because your natural state of being has been dampened or 'dimmed', and it feels dispirited, sad, chaotic, even restricted.

IMAGINATION, INTENTION & ATTITUDE

This is why having clear intention is so important. When your intentions are clear, you are able to dial up your innate energy field and direct this force to where you want it to go. But you first need that clarity of who you want to be and what you want to do. Otherwise, get distracted and lose focus, you lose the connection with your inner source of energy and enthusiasm. When you detach from your inner source, your energy saps, and your enthusiasm fades. You become dispirited and lack inspiration.

But when you remove all distractions and are focused, you tap into the limitless energy supply of your human spirit. You become 'in spirit', you become inspired. The key is to keep your mind as clear and as focussed as you can so that you can always tap into your natural source of power.

Psychologists, in fact, tell us that personal energy-management is the process of making conscious choices that support sustained energy, vitality, productivity, and inner calmness. The choices you make to sustain your energy levels on a consistent basis simply follow the Law of Cause and Effect. Your choices are the cause you set into motion, and your energy levels, vitality, productivity, and calmness are the desired result or effect.

Personal energy-management can therefore be summarised as a single word: *choice*.

Disregarding any chronic illness, your current mental and physical energy levels are the result of the personal and professional choices you have made up until this point in time. When I'm fitter, it's because I choose to go to the gym and exercise. When I'm unfit, it's because I choose to drive past the gym or spend the time watching a football game on TV. Or sleeping.

When I'm feeling healthier, it's because I choose to keep an eye on what I'm eating and drinking. When I'm feeling unhealthy, it's because I'm choosing sugary 'feel good' foods and choosing to ignore the amount of calories, cholesterol, and alcohol I ingest.

It's simple cause and effect: my choices affect my fitness and health, which ultimately affect my energy levels. Proper 'choice-making' is therefore a conscious process. It is a deliberate focus of your intentions to achieve a certain outcome. If your intention is to better manage your energy levels, then conscious choice-making is essential in achieving that intention.

In his 1906 published paper in *The Philosophical Review*, 'The Energies of Men', William James asserted that most people tend to give up on tasks and projects too soon. They usually give up before they get their 'second wind', he observed, which can propel them across the finish line.

James reckoned that we, as human beings, have stored-up reserves of energy that are ordinarily not called upon, but nonetheless exist and can be tapped into. We just need to keep digging and we'll find it. Unfortunately, he opined, most people never run far enough on their first wind to find out they've got a second.

> *Compared with what we ought to be, we are only half awake... We are making use of only a small part of our possible mental and physical resources.*

Good energy-management not only utilises your first wind, but also your second wind, which you will need to sustain your intentions and strengthen your will. A useful technique to help you with this is to identify your energy drains. Anything that drains your physical, mental, and emotional energy will also drain your vitality and motivation. Your resolve will weaken and your intentions will slip to the wayside.

Good energy-management will help you to limit your energy losses, which in turn will help you to maintain your forward momentum and progress in all aspects of your life.

Your 7 Life Segments: Energy-Management
Generally, there are seven common and typical segments that we all experience and in which we play a role throughout our life.

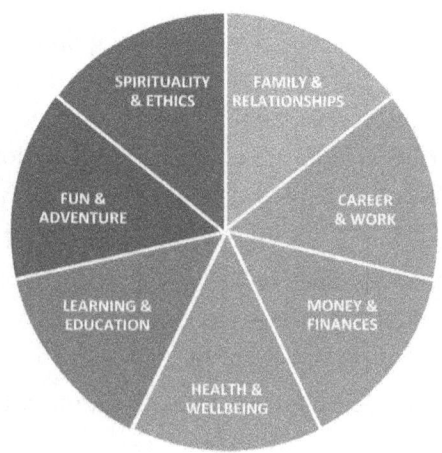

FIGURE 6: The 7 Life Segments

These '7 Life Segments' are interconnected pieces of a value circle that include:

1. Family & Relationships
2. Career & Work
3. Money & Finances
4. Health & Wellbeing
5. Learning & Education
6. Fun & Adventure
7. Spirituality & Ethics (or Religion & Morals)

These 7 Life Segments represent approximately 98-99% of most people's lives and are therefore a good representation of where our energy comes and goes throughout the day. Remember, personal energy-management is the result of making conscious choices that support sustained energy, vitality, productivity, and inner calmness. Here, then, is an energy-management exercise that you can do right now to evaluate any energy drains that might be slowing you down and affecting your day-to-day routine:

1. Identify where your energy is being siphoned off in each of these 7 key areas of your life: Family & Relationships, Career & Work, Money & Finances, Health & Wellbeing, Learning & Education, Fun & Adventure, Spirituality & Religion (or Morals & Ethics).
2. Next, review the list you've just made of your current energy drains and choose your Top Priority Items that you would most like to handle now.
3. Then decide which one you will action today and how you will do it.
4. Finally, write down how you plan to reduce your energy drains over the next 21 days.

Here are some examples of how to do this exercise:

Career & Work:

1. Energy drains: answering out of hours emails; gossip from colleagues about other colleagues; commuting times to work; skipping lunch breaks; working weekends; not taking annual holidays.
2. Priority: out of hours emails.
3. Action Plan: answer work emails at assigned times during the day e.g. first thing in the morning at work, and last thing in the evening before going home. Do not answer emails at any other time. This will help my energy-management and my time-management.

IMAGINATION, INTENTION & ATTITUDE

Health & Wellbeing:
1. Energy drains: poor sleep pattern; bad eating habits; too much alcohol; poor fitness; watching too much TV at night.
2. Priority: watching too much TV at night.
3. Action Plan: swap a TV program for a book. This will also improve my sleep pattern as reading also makes me sleepy.

The power of this exercise is setting your intention. Your intention determines where your energy flows. So once you identify your energy drains, make a written plan to reduce them, and then take action on that plan. You'll find not only that your energy levels begin to increase, but another remarkable discovery—your second wind.

P: Activate Project You

As we have mentioned, there are two main drivers that successful people align themselves with and identify as—the passion-driven swimmers, and the project-minded snipers.

Swimmers, as we've talked about, are the ones who immerse themselves in their lifelong creative bliss. Snipers, though, aren't so much passion driven as they are project minded. Their greatest joy is to immerse themselves in thoughtful endeavours. Where swimmers are right-brain creatives, snipers are left-brain thinkers.

Swimmers are centred in the moment of Now; snipers are focused on the future and how to get there. Snipers are goal orientated. Like football players, they kick goals. Like archers, they take aim at a target and make the shot. Where swimmers get lost in their passion, snipers find themselves in their projects. They like nothing more than to set themselves a goal, plan a route on how to get there, and then set forth toward that goal.

A sniper's happiness, joy and fulfilment is in the effort and journey toward their goal.

Snipers are like B.C. Forbes, the founder of *Forbes* magazine. They take on board his advice to build an air castle that the outside world cannot wreck.

It is when things go hardest, when life becomes most trying, that there is the greatest need for having a fixed goal, for having an air castle that the outside world cannot wreck. When few comforts come from without, it is all the more necessary to have a fount to draw from within. And the man or woman who has a star toward which to press cannot be thrown off the course, no matter how the world may try, no matter how far things seem to be wrong.

Snipers are project people. Their projects are their goals, their air castle, their star toward which they press and cannot be thrown off the course, even when weary. The goal to which a sniper is aiming helps to slice through the mind fog and part the haziness they've been trying to navigate through. It gives them clarity of the path ahead, the direction they need to take, and it gives them the confidence to strive down that path toward the destination they want to reach.

They also find they are filled with enthusiasm for the effort and work they need to do along the way. Even though they get tired, they are motivated to keep striving. Even though they get weary, their enthusiasm pushes them forward like the wind in a sail.

So it's important to identify your major goal in life. What is it that you want to be and do? What's your 'Project You'?

Here is another exercise that you can do right now to help you identify your 'Project You':

IMAGINATION, INTENTION & ATTITUDE

1. Who do you want to be when you grow up?
2. What do you want to achieve?
3. Why do you want to become that person and do what you want to do?
4. How do you plan on achieving that?

This exercise will help you identify the who, what, why, and how of Project You. Good advice is to think of how you can best serve others and your community, taking into account your strengths, personality, talents, and abilities. Through serving others you'll find your higher calling and your greatest purpose. Through serving others you'll find your enthusiasm and zest for life.

You'll find your Project You.

AWAKENING YOUR ATTITUDE SUPERPOWER

It's been said that attitude is the magic word.

This is because the right attitude, like imagination and intention, has superpower-like qualities. It can create a magical transformation in your life. It can transform anger into peace, frustration into calmness, failure into success.

But your Attitude superpower is a two-edged sword. It can work for you, and it can also work against you. The wrong attitude can keep you mired in frustration and failure. It can be the cause of much, if not all, your sufferings and privations. If you are currently experiencing loss, lack, and limitation in any form, or you simply fear a future in which you will experience loss, lack, and limitation, one of the best ways to turn your fortune around is through a change of attitude.

Life is a mirror. It reflects back to you everything you show it—your thoughts, emotions, words, and actions. Angry people tend to attract accidents and violence. Worrisome people tend to attract calamity and hardship. Happy people tend to attract luck and good fortune. This is the Law of Reflection in action, also known as karma.

What you put out, the universe reflects back to you.

As the computer geeks of the world like to say, "Garbage in, garbage out." They call it GIGO. That's because, despite their immense processing power, computers can only do what you tell them to do. They can only display the coding that's input. Bad coding gets bad results. Good coding gets good results.

Likewise, the universe is kind of like a gargantuan supercomputer. It works on the principle of GIGO and can only display the attitude that you input. Bad attitude gets bad results. Good attitude gets good results. This is why Earl Nightingale emphasised the importance of having the right attitude:

It is our attitude toward life that determines life's attitude toward us. We get back what we put out.

If you reject the world, the world will reject you. If you embrace the world, the world will embrace you. If you resent the world, the world will resent you. If you are happy with the world, the world will be happy with you. If you have no respect for the world, the world will have no respect for you. If you love the world, the world will love you.

This is also true of your inner world, the world that you inhabit in your mind. If you reject yourself, the outside world will also reject you. If you resent yourself, the outside world will also resent you. If you are happy with yourself, the outside world will be happy with you. If you have no respect for yourself, the outside world will have no respect for you. If you love yourself, the outside world will also love you.

IMAGINATION, INTENTION & ATTITUDE

Your attitude toward your inner world and your attitude to the outside world gets reflected back to you. Your attitude determines what you experience.

> *What you express to yourself and the outer world is returned express mail.*

I've never met the Williams sisters, Venus and Serena, the champion tennis players, nor have I watched the movie about their life, *King Richard*, but I remember hearing an anecdote about their time as younger tennis players under the coaching guidance of their father, Richard. From all accounts, they would spend hours and hours in training, hitting balls back and forth to one another with their father looking on and giving advice on their technique and game strategy. But the one thing he told the young girls over and over again was just one word: *attitude*.

Whenever he saw them making mistakes, or getting down on themselves, or getting frustrated and angry, he would call out across the court, "ATTITUDE!"

Then, if they slipped up again, he yelled, "ATTITUDE!"

That was it. That was all he had to say to get their mindset right and improve their play. Attitude helped them grow into the Grand Slam champions they became.

Serena and Venus reached the summit of their sport not just because they had great genetic talent, but because they had the right mental attitude. So did Michael Phelps, winner of 23 Olympic gold medals and arguably the greatest swimmer of all time, and this is his advice:

> *Are you going to wait until after you win your gold medal to have a good attitude? No. You're going to do it beforehand. You have to have the right mental attitude, and go from there. You're going to be an Olympic champion in attitude long before there's a gold medal around your neck.*

A good attitude isn't limited to success in sporting achievement, it's vital for success in any aspect of your life. You can have many roles in each of your 7 Life Segments and you can set just as many goals as you'd like to achieve. You can set family goals, career goals, money goals, health goals, even spiritual goals. But more than anything else, more than talent, skillset, luck, genetics, or your environment, your attitude will be the determining factor in your level of success in whatever you set out to achieve.

Zig Ziglar, motivational speaker and author of the bestselling book, *See You At The Top*,[14] put it this way:

> *Your attitude, not your aptitude, will determine your altitude.*

Imagine your Attitude superpower as the most powerful cell in your body, a stem cell. Stem cells are the formative cells for every organ in the human body. You have trillions of cells, every single one of which began its life as a stem cell and evolved through a series of pathways into the cell it is today—skin, brain, muscle, bone, hair, teeth, blood, kidney, liver, gut, nerve.

All cells in your body can trace their origins to a single stem cell. Which is why there is so much medical research into stem cells. Because of their adaptive nature, doctors and scientists hope to use stem cells as the ultimate 'silver bullet' to cure diseased and injured organs. For instance, by injecting harvested, healthy stem cells of a newborn baby into a damaged area of a paraplegic's spine, doctors hope to encourage the stem cells to form new nerve cells that can patch the severed spinal cord and heal it sufficiently for the patient to gain control of her legs and eventually walk again.

This is just one example. There is also hope that stem cells can someday help a patient's immune system to fight some types of cancers, such as lymphomas, leukaemias, and even

---

[14] *See You At The Top*, Zig Ziglar, Pelican Publishing Company, 1974

IMAGINATION, INTENTION & ATTITUDE

neuroblastomas[15]. Because of their innate ability to create any cell in the body, the potential use of stem cells is unlimited. So too your Attitude has unlimited potential.

Attitude sets the tone for your thoughts, emotions, words, and actions. Your attitude is the 'mind-cell' from which all your experience evolves.

That's why your Attitude is so powerful. Get it right, and everything else falls into place. Get it wrong, and everything falls apart. Your Attitude—your mind-cell—is the key to your success, or it is the key to your failure.

In his book, *Zen and the Art of Motorcycle Maintenance*,[16] Robert Pirsig discusses the importance of having the right attitude to get the results you want. Pirsig tells a group of friends of a set of instructions he has to assemble a Japanese bicycle, which begins, to the amusement of his friends, with these words, "Assembly of Japanese bicycle require great peace of mind."

This brings out chortles of laughter from his friends until they realise what great advice it is. There is a lot of wisdom in that instruction, Pirsig recounts, and goes on to explain (in the context of motorcycle maintenance) why this is so:

> *It's the whole thing. That which produces [peace of mind] is good maintenance; that which disturbs it is poor maintenance. That which we call workability of the machine is just an objectification of this peace of mind. The ultimate test's always your own serenity. If you don't have this when you start and maintain it while you're working you're likely to build your personal problems right into the machine itself.*

---

[15] A severe childhood cancer of the nerve cells near the adrenal gland.

[16] *Zen and the Art of Motorcycle Maintenance: An Inquiry into Values*, Robert Pirsig, William Morrow & Company, 1974

How many times have you built your personal problems right into the things you have done or are doing right now? How many times have you built your personal problems into your current project, your garden, your marriage, your career, your life, your health?

You see, to get a quality result you must first have a quality Attitude.

A State of Mind

An incident in London at the turn of the millennium highlights this point, or rather, the antithesis of this point. I required a set of shelving to be built in my Soho apartment and requested my landlord to send over his maintenance man to look into the job. A carpenter duly arrived the following Friday at 4:30pm. By his demeanour and curt introduction, I could tell he was in a rush.

After less than an hour, the carpenter packed his tool bag and headed out the front door saying the job was done. When I inspected the shelves, the bedroom was in a mess. Bits of wood and shavings littered the floor. The shelves themselves were roughly cut, with splintered edges and irregular cornering. I shook my head, as much for the state of workmanship as for the state of mind of the carpenter.

His attitude was to get the job done as quickly as possible and get out of there, probably to the local pub to meet his mates for Friday night drinks. He certainly didn't have a quality attitude. There was no pride in his work, and it showed in the lack of quality of his workmanship. He was in a rush to do the job and he didn't care for the results.

Thinking back on that incident, it was as if he actually resented having to do the job, and that resentment is what he built into the bedroom shelves. I doubt he had read *The Art of Motorcycle Maintenance*. I doubt he knew anything about getting your attitude right before you embark on a project, especially a project

IMAGINATION, INTENTION & ATTITUDE

that you're getting paid for and will affect other people. I doubt he knew that peace of mind is one such quality attitude.

But he isn't alone. We're all guilty of poor-quality workmanship in one form or another because we were rushed or had other things on our minds.

Yet the lesson is a vital one, and it's to first have peace of mind before you embark on anything you do. Then, with this attitude, you infuse that peace of mind into your thoughts, emotions, and actions, which assembles your experience of what you're doing and is built into the work you perform.

It's the whole thing, as Pirsig said. From the mind-cell of your Attitude grows everything else: your thoughts, your emotions, your actions, your workmanship. Your whole experience. In this Game of Life, you get back what you put out.

Your experience is an effect of your state of mind, not the other way around.

But how often do we seek peace of mind from the thing we are doing? How often do we look for happiness in external events or people or things? How often do we chase the pot of gold at the end of the rainbow?

Too often. Far too often.

And how successful are we at finding that peace of mind, or happiness, or pot of gold?

Probably not very much, if at all, and only then for a fleeting moment. Then we get up and begin the long, gruelling chase all over again.

No wonder we burn out in our 50s and 60s, just when we should really be enjoying the fruits of our labours. No wonder researchers tell us that the prevalence of anxiety and stress is the highest it's ever been in the Western world. Not to mention divorce rates, heart attacks, strokes, and addiction.

That's because we've got it the wrong way around. We've learned the wrong way of doing things. We've gotten into the wrong habit of expecting the world to give us what we want. We feel entitled to it. We even demand it. At worst, we fight and steal and kill for it.

But that's not how the universe works. That's not how life works. That's not how *you* work.

The universe will give you peace of mind *when you first have the attitude of peace of mind*.

Life will give you joy and happiness *when you first have the attitude of joy and happiness*.

You will find your pot of gold *when you first have the attitude of serving others and being generous of spirit*.

It all starts and ends with your "ATTITUDE!"

Success in a Bowl of Noodles

Of all the things I've been blessed to achieve in this lifetime—graduating as a medical doctor, travelling the world, becoming a husband and a father, writing many books, and more recently as a motivational speaker and mentor—I tell people that I found success in a bowl of noodles.

As a work-at-home father, I'm pretty busy. I also have three businesses, DoctorZed Publishing, my personal writing business, and my professional coaching business, 818: Unlocking Your Life. Because I work from my home office, I'm also responsible for the running of the house, which is probably another fulltime job in of itself. Needless to say, I reckon I'm one of the few males to have mastered the art of multitasking. I can cook the dinner, wash the clothes, help the kids do their homework, do the ironing, mow the lawn, chop firewood, and write this book all at the same time.

One evening, after spending an hour and a half cooking what I thought was a lovely Asian stir-fry, I felt my energy draining and my mood rapidly following it down the kitchen sink. After only

IMAGINATION, INTENTION & ATTITUDE

eating half their meal, my daughters pushed their unfinished bowl of noodles across the table, said thanks, and went back to their homework.

I stared at their leftovers and the big bowl of noodles that still remained to be eaten, thinking what a waste of time and effort. "Why do I bother?" I said to myself.

It was then that I realised it wasn't so much the end result that mattered, in this case the half-eaten stir-fry, but the attitude that I'd had when cooking the meal.

My intention had been good. I had wanted to make a meal that was enjoyable and tasty and different, and that attitude had been built into the meal. The fact that my daughters weren't hungry didn't detract from *the investment of myself* into the meal. In my heart I knew that I had given all I had into the preparing the dinner, and that was what mattered the most. I didn't need their approval. I didn't feel angry or upset. I didn't growl at them to eat every noodle in their bowl because there were kids starving in Africa (although why we say that to our kids, I'm not exactly sure). I actually felt at peace with the outcome.

So this is why I say I found success in a bowl of noodles, and what I discovered was this:

> *Success is dependent on how much of yourself you put into each and every moment.*

When you put yourself into each and every moment, you make this moment of Now bigger. You actively help the Universe to grow, and growth is the natural order of things.

When you put yourself into each and every moment, you make yourself bigger. You actively nurture yourself to grow, because what you put in you get out.

And how much you put into each moment is, in turn, dependent on your Attitude.

Which is why your Attitude determines your success.

4 IDENTITY, PURPOSE & CONVICTION

THE FORTUNA CODE

THE ROMAN GODDESS of fortune and success was Fortuna. She was the equivalent of the Greek goddess, Tyche. Although Fortuna has come to represent luck throughout the ages, and sometimes blind luck, as depicted by her statues wearing a blindfold, those in The 5% Club know that you make your own luck.

The Roman philosopher, Seneca (4BC - 65AD), was an advisor to the emperor Nero, and was a revered dramatist and poet. He spoke of an essential quality of fortune and success when he said:

> *Luck is what happens when preparation meets opportunity.*

What Seneca implied is that you are in control of your luck. This is because of two essential facts: first, you can control how you prepare; and second, you can control how vigilant you are to the opportunities that present themselves to you. Following this principle, here is the process of how you can start to make your own luck:

- -> Preparing for your fortune and success starts with the deliberate awakening of your superpowers of Imagination, Intention, and Attitude.
- -> Following this is the activation of your Identity ('I Am'), your Purpose ('I Will'), and your Conviction ('I Can') through the 4 Power Habits.

-> Each of these 4 Power Habits create a kind of alchemic Power Element, of which there are four: Faith, Valour, Value, Commitment.

-> These 4 Power Elements combined are the secret PIN to your fortune and success.

Let's decipher the Fortuna Code by first discussing how to align your Imagination, Intention, and Attitude.

IDENTITY: ALIGNING YOUR IMAGINATION AND INTENTION—I AM

Let's put this alchemic principle into practice and start by aligning your Imagination and Intention to create an identity of who you are and want to be—your 'I Am'.

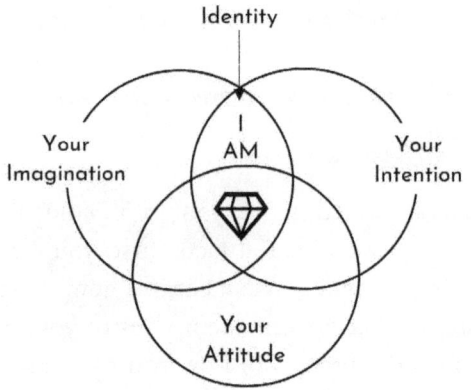

FIGURE 7:   Identity–I Am

'I Am!' is the most powerful statement of being there is. In fact, there is no other statement of being. Everything you think about yourself and explain who you are to others begins with, 'I Am.'

I Am... a teacher, doctor, lawyer, banker, bus driver, student, cleaner, husband, wife, mother, father, brother, sister.

IDENTITY, PURPOSE & CONVICTION

I Am… Australian, American, European, African, Asian, Arabian, Indian, Polynesian, Latino, citizen of the earth.

I Am… a warrior, lover, activist, hippy, musician, footballer, baseballer, priest, rabbi, imam, writer, ballerina, artist, soul of the world, child of God.

Everything begins with who you are, your 'I Am'. From you arises all your thoughts, dreams, hopes, desires. From you arises the beginning of all inspiration and motivation for being the person you want to be and doing the things you want to do. From you arises your purpose and meaning, as well as all the plans and strategies and mechanics of how you can be and do what you want.

Your 'who' is the foundation upon which your 'what', 'why', and 'how' is built.

As we have discussed, your outer world reflects your inner world, so it's up to you to make your inner world as great as you can by defining who you are. So, how do you see yourself? How do you want others to see you? What do you want to be famous for?

Here are some examples of how you can use your imagination and intention to define who you are in the context of being and doing.

'I AM BEING…'			
Safe	Creative	Love	Free
Powerful	Abundant	Happy	Awakened
Strong	Empowered	Expressive	Peaceful
Sensual	Wise	Kind	Connected
Healthy	Worthy	Generous	Eternal

TABLE 3:   'I Am' Statement-Being

'I AM DOING...'			
Son/Daughter	Parent	Partner	Friend
Assistant	Carer	Financier	Tradie
Employee	Employer	Entrepreneur	Retired
Sports person	Healer	Philanthropist	Volunteer
Mentor/coach	Traveller	Writer	Artist
Advocate	Politician	Defence force	Scientist
Religious leader	Community leader	Farmer/producer	Social worker
Activist	Trainer	Teacher	Builder

TABLE 4: 'I Am' Statement–Doing

Who and what you are is whatever you set your Imagination and Intention to.

Remember, though, you are bigger than you think you are. You are bigger than the things you do, and you are bigger than the identity you assume. You are the awareness behind your thoughts, the awareness of 'I Am' from which all your thoughts of 'I Am' arise.

PURPOSE: ALIGNING YOUR INTENTION AND ATTITUDE—I WILL

We recently discussed how to awaken your Intention by giving yourself a regular 'PEP talk'. Through the activation of your Passion, Energy-management systems, and Project You, your Intention superpower is roused from its slumber. Your Intention, aligned with your Attitude superpower, delivers a supercharged boost to your motivation and drive—your 'I Will!'

IDENTITY, PURPOSE & CONVICTION

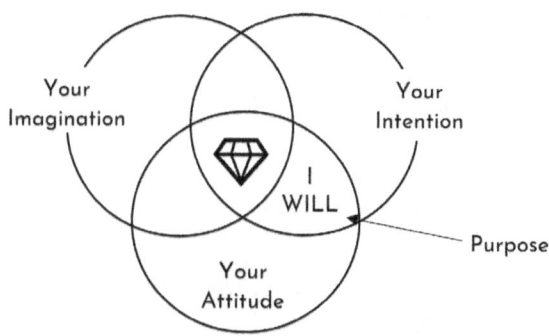

FIGURE 8: Purpose–I Will

Purpose is important because it gives meaning to who you are and what you do, as well as sparking your motivation and drive. For instance, your intention to fulfill a role that is coupled and aligned with a positive attitude toward fulfilling the role will give meaning to that role and motivate you to fulfill that role. Your intention to do a task that is coupled and aligned with a positive attitude toward completing that task will give meaning to that task and motivate you to do that task.

Any depletion of intention or attitude, however, will deplete your motivation because your purpose is depleted. You won't be motivated to fulfill a particular role, nor will you be motivated to complete a particular task.

In the past, parents, partners, teachers, bosses, and community leaders, even strangers, have probably tried to motivate you to act in a certain way, or to behave in a certain way, or to complete certain chores or tasks. They probably would have either used the stick or carrot approach. They would have tried to threaten you with extra work, or violence, or incarceration, or penalised you, or withheld something from you, even threaten to do something you wouldn't want to happen if you didn't do what they asked.

That's the stick approach, using pain as a motivator, as opposed to the carrot approach, where they would have tried to entice you with something pleasurable. Maybe money, or food, or a nice treat, or a bribe of some kind. It's seduction of some sort.

Some people will even try to manipulate you through emotions, making you feel guilty, or jealous, or angry, or other negative emotions. Others will try to use more positive emotions to manipulate you, like making promises they know they'll never keep, giving you false hope, lying to you that they love you.

But manipulation through pleasure and pain, carrot and stick, is not motivation. True motivation can only come through the purpose and meaning you give to something. True motivation is internal, not external. As a general rule, there are three main purpose-driven, motivating factors:

1. Assuredness: the belief you are doing what is right.
2. Free will: the belief that you have the power to make right choices.
3. Payoff: the belief that you will benefit from doing what is right.

You can only feel truly motivated when you believe what you are doing is the right thing to do, when you feel you are empowered to make decisions without coercion, and when you believe you will be rewarded for your efforts. You will certainly not be motivated if you feel what you're doing is the wrong thing for you, when you feel coerced to make decisions, or you think you won't be rewarded for all the effort you will put in.

So any motivation that is going to have significant impact and last for an extended period of time has to come through the purpose you assign. It cannot come from the outside, not matter how much pain is threatened or pleasure is promised. It can only come through you and you alone. This you do by activating and aligning your Intention with your Attitude to create an inner motivating force, your 'I Will'.

Your 'I Will' helps set your purpose for being who you are as

IDENTITY, PURPOSE & CONVICTION

well as setting the purpose for doing what you do. The greater your sense of 'I Will', the greater your sense of purpose. The greater your sense of purpose, the greater your motivation to achieving what you want to achieve.

CONVICTION: ALIGNING YOUR ATTITUDE AND IMAGINATION—I CAN

After defining the identity of who you want to be and determining what you want to achieve ('I Am'), and after establishing your inner sense of purpose and motivation to achieve these things ('I Will'), the next step is to tap into your self-belief to galvanise your momentum and progress. This you do by aligning your Attitude and Imagination to supercharge your conviction and direction ('I Can').

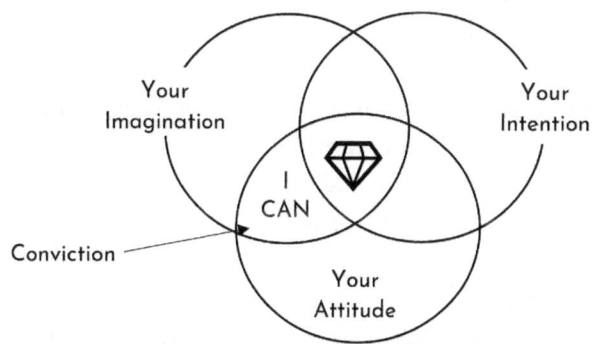

FIGURE 9:   Conviction–I Can

One of the tell-tale predictive signs of future success is conviction. Not the legal conviction of being found guilty of a crime, but the conviction that you are doing the right thing and heading in the right direction. The conviction that you know what you are doing. The conviction that you know how to do what you need to do. The conviction that you are the right person for the job at hand. The conviction that you are going to the right place.

Conviction arises from being convinced, to be free of doubt. When you are convinced, you go beyond belief; you have a knowing, an absolute certainty. A knowing certainty, not about the world, but about who you are, what you do, and where you're going. This kind of knowing certainty is like an alpine mountain, an immoveable force. This is where the strength or power of conviction stems from, when you are convinced that there is nothing else you should be, when you are convinced that there is nothing else you should be doing. When you are convinced that there is no other destination than the one to which you are heading, you are utterly convinced of the value of who you are and your role in the world. The truth is who you are, and who you are is the truth. An immoveable force.

The power of conviction is twofold: it fires your passion, and it builds resilience. Conviction sparks a flame that can burn for years, even decades. It's the fuel that keeps your light burning when there seems nothing but darkness and the end seems so far away.

Conviction also helps you to overcome obstacles and nullify resistance, both internal and external, which allows you to be resilient and to persevere when challenges arise.

The power of conviction—sparking passion, overcoming obstacles, nullifying resistance—is a key factor in achieving the results you want to achieve. But people with weak conviction have weak passion and weak resolve. Their energy runs low very quickly, they don't persevere, and they give up at the first sign of trouble. Because of this, they don't arrive at the destination where they wanted, instead ending up in a place they probably never imagined. They end up in a job they never wanted, doing things they never thought they would, living in a house they didn't want, and becoming somebody unrecognisable to themselves.

Animals can teach us about this power of conviction and being true to who you are. Prior to COVID-19, I became the father to three orphaned roosters. The owner of these chickens was moving house and their new landlord wasn't allowing any pets, especially roosters. There weren't too many other options, besides the chopping block, so I agreed to look after them, much to the bemusement of my family and neighbours. I soon learned that roosters don't just crow at the break of dawn, they crow the whole day. They crow loudly, and they crow often. Very loudly, and very often.

One afternoon just after lunchtime, I discovered the roosters perched on the outside dining table at the back of the house. They didn't see me coming and they didn't detect my presence. All three were throwing their heads to the sky and crowing with delight, just because they could. Just because they were roosters.

In that moment I sensed that they were just being what they were born to be, roosters. Nothing more, nothing less. They were just being who they were, and taking absolute pleasure and enjoyment in doing so.

I didn't disturb them. I just let them do what they wanted to do, crow for their hearts' delight, and continued to watch them, thinking that here was the secret to a happy and joyful life:

> *You just have to be who you are and do what you were born to do. Nothing more. Nothing less.*

Animals, including roosters, don't need convincing of this. They don't need to be convinced that they should be anything other than who they are. They are who they are and that's it. Animals know this. Roosters know this. But humans don't.

We complicate our lives so much that we have forgotten who we are. So many things fill our heads that we forget how to be human. So many thoughts, worries, fears fill our minds that we forget how to crow to our hearts' delight.

So we need to wipe away the doubts and fears and get crystal clear on who we are. When we do, we will see ourselves in a new light. We will understand ourselves differently. We will gain a knowing certainty of who we really are and what we must do, and we will take absolute enjoyment in doing so.

That's the power of conviction.

*　*　*

We will now discuss in depth how to awaken your superpowers of Imagination, Intention, and Attitude so that you can build the Power Elements of Faith, Valour, Value, and Commitment through the discipline and development of the 4 Power Habits of Success:

SUPERPOWER	ALIGNMENT	POWER HABIT	POWER ELEMENT
IMAGINATION + INTENTION	IDENTITY (I AM)	#1: SELF-ASSUREDNESS & SELF-BELIEF	FAITH
INTENTION + ATTITUDE	PURPOSE (I WILL)	#2: COURAGE & CONFIDENCE	VALOUR
		#3: OTHER PEOPLE THINKING	VALUE
ATTITUDE + IMAGINATION	CONVICTION (I CAN)	#4: PLANNING, PREPARATION & PERSEVERANCE	COMMITMENT

TABLE 5: The Fortuna Code

PART II

POWER HABIT #1

SELF-ASSUREDNESS & SELF-BELIEF

POWER ELEMENT #1

FAITH

5 THE POWER OF FAITH

BUILDING YOUR FAITH MUSCLE

ONE OF THE most striking features of people who exude success, and who others aspire to emulate, is their self-assuredness. They have an air of certainty and belief in themselves. They seem to lack any self-doubt or insecurities. With an eye on the future, they are focused on what they want to achieve and aren't anchored to their failures in the past.

They are the ones who others say, "They know where they're going."

Yet hope as we might, just as there's no magic wand you can wave to instantly transform your body into a fit, athletic, muscular physique, there is no magic wand to increase your self-assuredness and self-belief. Some genetics do come into play, but generally your fitness and physique is a result of discipline and the habit of regular exercise. So too with self-assuredness and self-belief—it requires regular mental exercise.

Although success is multifactorial and differs from person to person, there are common fundamentals that you can replicate and make part of your day-to-day routine. As we've just discussed in the previous section, these fundamentals are Identity ('I Am'), Purpose ('I Will'), and Conviction ('I Can').

In this chapter, we will be expanding on these fundamentals and discussing how they can be used to build the Power Element of Faith through the first Power Habit of Self-Assuredness & Self-Belief.

These are the three components we will discuss:

#1: Identity: Clarifying your *vision* of who you are—I Am!

#2: Purpose: Amplifying your *intent*—I Will!

#3: Conviction: Reinforcing your self-*belief*—I Can!

To clarify, the faith we will be discussing is the faith of self-assuredness and self-belief. This is the faith in who you are and what you are doing, including faith in your purpose and direction. We won't be discussing religious faith, although identity, purpose, and conviction are very strong components of religious faith. Both types of faith, personal and religious, require regular attention and nurturing to maintain strength and durability. Without attention and nurture, faith withers and dies.

As the American Indian parable goes:

Inside you two wolves are constantly in battle: Fear and Faith. Which one wins is the one you feed.

You feed the wolf of fear by giving it attention. You feed the wolf of faith by giving it attention. One is the wolf of failure. The other is the wolf of success. What you feed is strengthened. What you give regular attention and nurture to is strengthened.

Attention and nurture are the equivalent of regular workouts at the gym. All three components—I Am (Vision), I Will (Intent), I Can (Belief)—build and strengthen your faith muscle by constant repetition and discipline. The opposite is also true. Failure to achieve your desired outcomes is a common result of a weak or atrophied faith muscle. Failure commonly follows those who have mind fog and no clear vision of what they want, or even who they want to be. Failure commonly follows those who are more certain of failure than they are of success. Failure also tends to follow those who are lacking in the self-belief department.

So the first step to transform your life into success is to build and strengthen your faith muscle, and this you do by activating your Imagination, Intention, and Attitude to develop the essential components of Identity, Purpose, and Conviction: 'I Am! I Will! I Can!'.

It's like a mantra: "I Am! I Will! I Can!" The more you repeat it in the gymnasium of your mind, the stronger your faith muscle becomes.

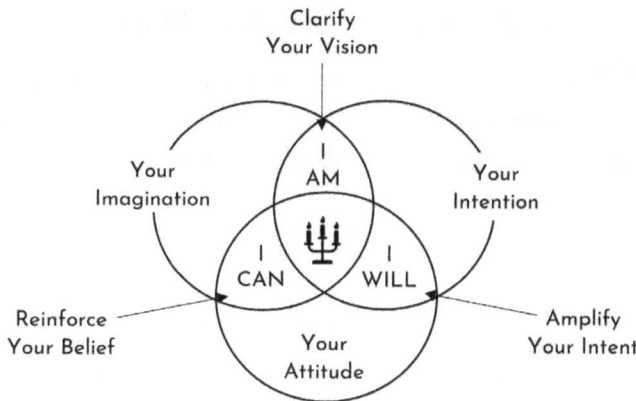

FIGURE 10: Power Element–Faith

The above diagram explains how your Imagination, Intention, and Attitude align to build your faith muscle:

-> Identity: the overlap where your Imagination and Intention align is where you focus and *clarify your vision*—your 'I Am'.

-> Purpose: the overlap where your Intention and Attitude align is where you *amplify your intent* and build your certainty—your 'I Will'.

-> Conviction: the overlap where your Attitude and Imagination align is where you *reinforce your self-belief* and know that you can be and do anything you set your mind to—your 'I Can'.

The power of who you want to be and what you want to do is in the central overlap where the three components of Vision (I Am), Intent (I Will), and Self-Belief (I Can) merge and align as one Power Element called Faith.

The Power Habit of Self-Assuredness & Self-Belief is how you develop this Power Element.

IDENTITY: CLARIFYING YOUR VISION—I AM

In our discussion on awakening your Imagination superpower, we learned that 'I Am' is the most powerful statement of being there is. So don't think small. Don't be small.

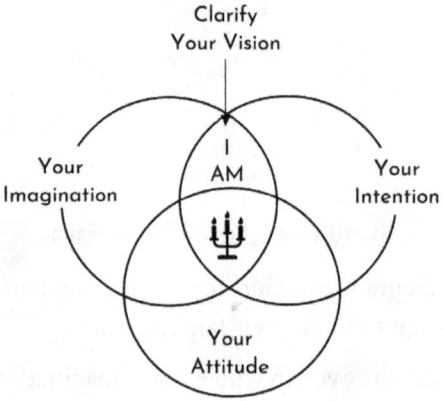

FIGURE 11:   Clarify Your Vision–I Am

Small-minded thinking is disabling and self-limiting. When your 'I Am' is identified with a small, limited sense of being, you disable yourself as much as you would if you wore a blindfold and tried to walk with your shoelaces tied together. You stumble forward. You don't know which direction to take. You don't know what you should do next. You keep bumping into things and making a mess.

One day, or even one week, of this would seem bad enough, but imagine spending your entire life in this state. Imagine spending your entire life thinking you're small, limited, isolated, and powerless. Unfortunately, this is a common reality for most people. More often than not, though, the underlying issue is not our lack of ability or our lack of knowhow, but our clarity of vision. Specifically, the clarity of vision of who and what we are.

But what blindfolds us? What gets in the way of seeing clearly? What prevents us from having 20/20 vision?

The parable of *The Pastor's Wife* gives us a clue.

> Every weekend, a pastor's wife noticed the next-door neighbour hanging out her bedsheets on the clothesline. But every weekend the sheets were stained and dirty.
>
> "What's going on over there?" the pastor's wife asked her husband. "Her sheets are always filthy."
>
> The pastor looked through the kitchen window beyond the fence to the next-door neighbour's clothesline, saying nothing.
>
> Again, the same thing happened the following weekend. The pastor's wife, noticing the sheets on the neighbour's clothesline, shook her head and complained at how filthy the sheets were. Again the pastor said nothing.
>
> The same thing also happened the following weekend. And again. And again. And again, until the pastor decided to do something about it. Before the neighbour hung out her bedsheets the following weekend, the pastor filled up his bucket, propped his ladder against the kitchen window, then wiped away the dust and the grime that had accumulated from the rain and wind.

Later that day, the pastor's wife looked across at the neighbour's clothesline, and said, "Oh, look, the neighbours must have bought a new washing machine. Their bedsheets are sparkling clean."

* * *

The dust and grime on our windows to the outside world is our constant mental chatter.

The negative thoughts that churn in our head, the resentments, the judgements, the fears, the hatreds, the angers, the jealousies, the gossips, the worries, the vanities, the wants, the desires, the rejections, the shames, the blames, the never being good enoughs. These are the things that smudge our eyes. These are the things we must wipe away before we can see clearly.

But why should we care? Why should it matter whether or not we see clearly?

Because those who are crystal clear on who they are, what they want to do, why they do it, and how they do it are far more successful than those who don't have that clarity. They are far more successful than the small-minded ones who see the world and themselves through dirty and dusty windows.

In talking with clients about developing a clear vision and thinking bigger, I'm often surprised at the resistance to 'cleaning their windows'. There are many instances where clients have challenged my advice with a gruff, 'Why do I need it?'

It's just their way of saying, 'I don't get it,' or 'I don't see the point,' so here are the main benefits of 'cleaning your windows' and having clear vision:

1. Laser Focus—to intensify your desire and self-confidence.
2. Awareness—to regain control of the controllables.
3. Resilience—to keep persevering and win the battle.

THE POWER OF FAITH

#1: Laser Focus

The power of a laser is achieved through the intense concentration of light rays onto a single point of focus. Lasers can cut through metal, which is amazing when you consider that a laser is just a beam of light. Likewise, when you have clarity of vision, your thoughts and intention become so focused it can seem as though you have the power to cut through metal, like a laser beam.

The power of having laser focus is that it gives you the direction, motivation, and engagement to achieve the results you are after:

1. Direction—your vision cuts through the mind fog and points you in the direction of your intended destination.
2. Motivation—your focus gives you the determination and drive to keep moving forward, no matter what obstacles appear on your path.
3. Engagement—where vision gives direction and motivation creates drive, engagement gives you the commitment to continue walking your path and staying the course.

Lack of focus, by contrast, means you will wander lost and directionless, you will lack the energy and motivation to keep going, and you will become disengaged with what you are doing. As Brian Tracy, motivational speaker and author of *Eat That Frog!*,[17] said:

> *Single-minded concentration in the direction of your dreams intensifies your desires and increases your self-confidence.*

---

[17] *Eat that Frog!*, Brian Tracey, Berrett-Koehler, 2001

When you have clear vision, your focus sharpens into that 'single-minded concentration' that is a pre-requisite for success and prosperity.

That's the power of laser focus. That's your power.

#2: Awareness

There are always things beyond your control, yet having a clear vision goes a long way to helping you control the controllables and regain control over your circumstances.

The things you can control are the dirt and the grime on your windows to the outside world. To focus on these things is to see a stained view. So to change what you see, focus instead on what you can control, your controllables. This is how you wipe clean your window and see a clear view.

Members of The 5% Club focus on what they can control and don't worry so much about what they can't control. They feel empowered because they feel they can influence certain things in their life, which gives them a sense of control and stability. Those that struggle the most in life, however, tend to get caught up in what they can't control and forget about what they can control. They feel disempowered because they feel they have no influence over most of the things that happen around them, which gives them a sense of ineffectiveness and instability.

Some time after I swapped my stethoscope for the pen and embarked on my new career as a writer in 2000, I read an article that discussed the main difference between an amateur or hobby writer and a professional writer. Amateur or hobby writers, the article pointed out, only write when they are in the mood to write. They only write when the circumstances are right and they feel like writing. Professional writers, in contrast, write every day irrespective of whether they feel like it or whether circumstances are conducive to writing. A professional writer will write whether or not she is in the mood.

At the time, it was good advice, and it still is. There are many days when I don't feel in the mood to write, but I always remember what this article said and it motivates me to do at least some writing every day. The weather outside, good or bad, hot or cold, is not within my control. Family crises, like my children getting injured or being sick, are not within my control. Unexpected events, like car breakdowns or electricity outages, are not within my control. I can complain as much as I like that circumstances are not ideal for writing. I can complain that I'm not in the mood for writing today, but whether I sit down at the keyboard and write is within my control. How much I write is within my control. My intention to write something every day is within my control.

Another aspect of writing that writers can, and must, control is self-criticism and self-judgement. Doubting whether your writing is any good, or doubting whether anybody will read your writing, is the fastest way to stop tapping the keyboard. As a writer, you have to overcome your doubts and fears of not being good enough, otherwise you'll stop writing. A writer who doesn't write is not a writer, she is an ex-writer, like an ex-smoker, someone who thinks about it a lot but simply doesn't do it anymore.

Writers therefore need to control how they think about themselves and their writing. Writers also need to let go of what readers will think about their writing. They need to stop hoping that 100% of their readers will love their work, and instead embrace the 3:3:3 principle.[18] This principle states that 33% of readers will hate what the author writes, 33% will not care either way, and 33% will love what the author writes. So all writers need do is to focus on the 33% that will love what they write and not worry about the others who will never like their writing or those who will never be bothered either way.

---

[18] I often refer to this as the 'Drew Barrymore Principle', after reading what the actress, Drew Barrymore, said to an interviewer about the advice her brother gave in dealing with hateful reviewers and critics.

THE POWER OF YOU!

It's a great principle to stick to in any aspect of life. Despite the inherent need to be loved by everyone on the planet, it isn't going to happen. Not everyone is going to love you, no matter how nice a person you are. Even the most lovable human being to ever exist was hated and crucified. So where does that leave you?

It leaves you to control what you can control, which is what you think of yourself. As much as you'd like to, you can't control what other people think of you. Peter Brock (1945-2006) was a legendary Australian racing driver for over 40 years, and he is considered one of the greatest ever. He won Australia's pinnacle touring car event, The Bathurst 1000, nine times, earning him the title of 'King of the Mountain'. He was a multiple winner of other major endurance races, the winner of the Australian Touring Car Championship three times, and he was inducted into the V8 Supercars Hall of Fame in 2001.

Unfortunately, some of his great achievements on the track were tarnished by his offroad detours away from the track. But when asked about the criticism he had received for his extramarital affair and the damage it had done to his reputation, Peter Brock told the reporter something that would do every person well to take to heart. He said, "What other people think of me is none of my business."

A racing car driver learns very quickly that there are many things that cannot be controlled. Accidents can happen. Punctures can happen. Engines can blow. Rain can fall. Fuel can run out. Brakes can fail. Other drivers can crash into you. So there's no point in worrying about what you can't control. You won't get off the starting grid if you are worried about all the things that could go wrong. All you can do is control what you can control.

This includes what happens off the track in your everyday life, including what other people think of you. Here are some other examples of what you can and can't control:

CAN CONTROL	CAN'T CONTROL
How you respond to external events and stimuli.	The weather.
What you think of yourself.	What other people think of you.
Your money and budget.	The economy.
What you eat and drink.	What other people eat and drink.
Your actions and behaviour.	Other people's actions and behaviour.
Your beliefs.	Other people's beliefs.
How you drive.	The traffic.
Your work ethic and attitude.	Your job or your boss.
Your love for others.	Other people's love for you.

TABLE 6: What You Can & Can't Control

So awareness of what you can control, and awareness of what you can't control, will go a long way to determine whether you cross the finishing line and see the chequered flag, or if you get stuck on the starting grid of life.

#3: Resilience

Have you ever noticed that some people can stick to a task or a mission while others fall to the wayside?

There are those who give up easily, and there are those who keep moving forward despite the odds against them. No matter what happens, no matter what obstacles they encounter along the way, they keep moving forward. Nothing else matters. Only moving toward the intended outcome is important.

Part of that resilience comes from having a clear vision of what's required to be done to achieve what they want to achieve.

It's like having tunnel vision, with only the goal ahead in sight. Without this vision, it's easy to get distracted and side-tracked. When this happens, procrastination sets in and resilience falls away. Great leaders know this. They therefore give their community a great vision. They stick to that vision even when all else seems to be failing. They give hope.

Poor leaders, though, don't know this. They don't have vision. They are reactionary and short-sighted. They rarely instil hope to their community, so the people get disillusioned and stop following them.

One of the greatest World War 2 POW movies ever made, *The Great Escape*, is a tale of great leadership, resilience, and hope. Based on the book of the same name by Paul Brickhill,[19] this 1963 classic begins three years into the war in 1942. The Nazis have decided to round up their most troublesome Allied POWs and imprison them in a new, state of the art, escape-proof camp, the dreaded Stalag Luft III. Upon arrival, the new inmates waste no time making a few impromptu escape attempts. These escape attempts are predictably unsuccessful, with the hero, Steve McQueen, ending up in solitary confinement on several occasions.

But it is the arrival of Roger Bartlett, designated 'Big X,' played by Richard Attenborough, who elevates the escape attempts to the next level. He takes charge of a committee devoted to planning escapes and he immediately sets to work on organising the biggest breakout ever executed in the history of POW camps. His vision is to break out 250 POWs from the camp through the construction of three tunnels.

This is certainly no easy task, but he is determined to succeed. The prisoners begin digging the tunnels, appropriating building

---

[19] Brickhill was an Australian fighter pilot who was a prisoner at the actual Stalag Luft III in Poland, where the story is set.

THE POWER OF FAITH

materials to support the tunnels from collapsing, sewing civilian clothing, even forging documents for when they escape into German territory. Their efforts are fraught with mishaps, tunnel collapses, and the problem of hiding all the dirt they are excavating from underground. At one stage, one of the tunnels is discovered by the camp guards, forcing the prisoners to hasten their escape through one of the other tunnels. Of the original 250 men chosen to escape, only 76 make it out. Of these 76 escapees, 73 are recaptured. Of these 73 who are recaptured, 50 are shot.[20] In the movie, only three of the original 250 POWs manage to get away, a Pole, a Brit, and an Australian.[21]

The Great Escape is a story of real-life success on many levels. On one level, although three men successfully escaping and evading the German authorities out of an initial total of 250 might not seem like an overall success, it has been estimated that up to 5 million Germans were involved in searching for the escapees at any one point. This is a significant number pulled away from the war effort that couldn't be directed to assist on the battlefield.

On another level, it's a success story of ingenuity, planning, and logistics. It's literally a story of tunnel vision. Of setting a vision, communicating that vision, implementing that vision, and seeing it through to the very end.

But on its highest level, it's a story of triumph over adversity, of good over evil, of right over wrong. It's a story of persisting when the odds are against you, of enduring despite the setbacks, of pushing through even when the walls collapse on top of you. It's a success story of leadership.

You may or you may not ever be in a position of leadership at work or in a team environment, but you will always be in a position

---

[20] Which actually happened in the real break out, but not as portrayed in the movie in one shooting scene that kills all 50 men at once.

[21] In the real breakout in 1942, it was two Norwegians and a Dutchman, all flyers with the British Royal Airforce.

of self-leadership. This is why you need to be a great self-leader and have, to some extent, tunnel vision. You need to stay true to your cause despite the setbacks. You need to keep digging to reach your goal. You need to remain clear on who you are, what you want, why you do it, and how to achieve it. Otherwise you'll get disillusioned and you'll stop digging.

You'll stop following your dream, and you will never have your great escape.

Knowing Thyself

As the story of *The Great Escape* shows us, success follows those who have clear vision. In our day-to-day life, this translates to a clear vision of who you are and what you want to achieve. This means knowing who you are now and who you want to be. Successful people know the importance of this, and they make a habit of continually defining who they are and identifying their 'I Am'.

You therefore need to get to know yourself and to know yourself well. Here is an exercise you can do to get to the core of your 'I Am', which, if you're struggling to get a clear picture of who you are and who you want to be, I thoroughly recommend. It's a psychology-based exercise that I call, 'Knowing Thyself', and it's simply this:

1. Get a pen and paper and sit down somewhere quiet where you won't be disturbed for 30 minutes.
2. Write a list of numbers 1-20 down the page.
3. Next to each number, write the words "I am…"
4. Starting at No.1, describe who you are by completing each of the 20 statements "I am…"

Use the 7 Life Segments we've previously discussed as an aid to writing your list. You'll find the first 10 statements relatively easy. The next 5 statements are moderately more difficult, and the last 5 statements will be the most difficult and take the most amount of thought and time to complete. But by the end of the exercise, you will have 20 statements about yourself that all begin with the powerful words, 'I Am'.

Now for the hardest part. Of all 20 statements about you, is there one single word that represents the totality of who you are and who you want to be? A kind of umbrella word that captures the essence of you? Is there one word that you can identify with and claim it as your own?

For example, my 1-word is *prescriber*. It defines in all aspects—doctor, author, mentor, motivational speaker—who I have been, who I am now, and who I want to be. I like this word 'prescriber' because I want to be somebody who helps you to prescribe your future. It also has that lovely word 'scribe' as part of it. I use this as my 1-word 'identity badge' because it succinctly and efficiently describes everything about me: who I am, what I do, why I do it, and how I do it.

Now, it took me about 12 months of determination and constant thinking to find this word, even though it was staring me right in the face for a long time. The point is, finding your 1-word will take effort on your behalf, but it will certainly be worth your while, and, in any case, just be sure it isn't already staring you in the face.

6 CERTAINTY & KNOWING

PURPOSE: AMPLIFYING YOUR INTENT—I WILL

FAILURES HAPPEN AS much to successful people as they do to unsuccessful people. Probably more, because successful people keep trying no matter what and it's only natural the more you try the more you'll fail. The more you swing, the more you'll miss. But you'll also succeed more too.

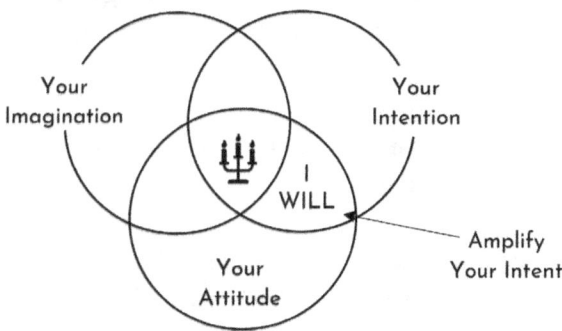

FIGURE 12:   Amplify Your Intent–I Will

The master has failed more times than the beginner has even tried, as the saying goes. As such, success is by and large a numbers game. The more you understand this, the more you'll succeed. It's called 'The Law of Averages'.

George Herman "Babe" Ruth, one of the most famous names in US baseball history, was someone who epitomised The Law of Averages. He was the first person to hit 60 home runs in a season and is considered the greatest baseballer of all time. Babe Ruth was someone who wasn't afraid to strike out, and his attitude of 'Keep swinging!' and, 'Every strike brings me closer to the next home run,' helped the NY Yankees to many titles.

When interviewed after one famous, series-clinching game against Philadelphia, he was asked what was going through his mind when 0-2 at the plate and facing defeat. He is reputed as saying something along the lines of: "I knew if I kept swinging, the Law of Averages would work in my favour."

Babe Ruth had immense faith in his abilities as a hitter and, just as importantly, he also had faith in the Law of Averages. As long as he kept swinging, he was confident the Law of Averages would ensure the results would eventually fall in his favour. Likewise, if you want to succeed you just have to keep trying. You just have to keep swinging. You just have to keep working at it until you achieve the results you're after. And there you have it, the master-word, which is 'work'.

People who succeed not only have great faith, they have a great work ethic.

People who succeed want to work. They love to work. They love to keep swinging, to keep giving it a shot. They have a great attitude to work. They keep trying because they know where they're going. They also know that to get there they have to keep putting in effort, thus allowing The Law of Averages to work in their favour.

As we know, faith without works is dead. It's no surprise then, that people who give up and fail generally don't make the most of The Law of Averages. They don't have a great work ethic. In fact, they actually have a work phobia, a fear of doing work (which is called 'ergophobia' or 'ponophobia').

They have a poor attitude to work because they generally don't know what they want or where they're going, so the return on investment isn't there for them. It just isn't worth the effort. It

CERTAINTY & KNOWING

isn't worth the effort because they focus on the misses, the strikes, not the hits. Imagine if Babe Ruth only focused on his strikes. He would never have summoned the effort to keep swinging, he would never have hit 700+ home runs, and the world of baseball would have missed out on the greatest player to stand at the plate.

Thankfully, he had a success attitude, not a failure attitude. For Babe Ruth, his attitude determined his altitude, as Zig Ziglar would have said.

Attitude is the magic word. But it isn't too difficult, nor do you require magic, to change a failure attitude to a success attitude if you want to: it's more or less a simple exercise in perspective. It can be as simple as looking at things from a different angle, which can be all the difference in succeeding or failing.

But what is a failure attitude? What is the difference between the attitude of success and the attitude of failure?

From my experience, a failure attitude is any mindset or thought processing that encompasses any or all of the following:

1. Blame—blaming others, the situation, lack of money, know-how, or resources, or anything else other than yourself for your failures, and the refusal to acknowledge your part in the result or situation you find yourself in.

2. Losing first, winning second—believing that you are already going to lose or not succeed before you've even started, and that any wins you might achieve are the result of good luck rather than good performance.

3. Excuse making—being more invested in why you failed or why you lost than what you can do to find a solution and succeed.

4. Mediocrity—accepting less than the best, both from yourself and from others, but mainly from yourself and what you are capable of being and achieving. Mediocrity is nothing less than the refusal to utilise your talents and maximise your potential in order to become the person you're capable of becoming.

5. Entitlement—believing the world owes you a living and all you have to do is sit back and wait for the good things to come your way without you having to do anything.

So what do you need to do to change these failure traits into success traits?

It's not too difficult, actually. There is an antidote to each of these five failure traits, but you'll need to keep working on them day after day until they become positive, intentional character traits. These five antidotes to a failure attitude are:

1. Be Response-able.
2. Win First, Learn Second.
3. Be Solution Focused.
4. Think BIG.
5. Be a Person of Value.

#1: Be Response-able

The game of soccer is considered the most popular game on the planet. More people play soccer and watch soccer than any other game. More than basketball, more than cricket, more than tennis, more than rugby. But there is another game that is, in fact, even more popular than soccer—the blame game.

Everybody, at least once in their life, I'm sure, has actively participated in the blame game. Not just as a spectator on the sidelines watching what was going on, but as a fully committed player. Maybe even one of the best players on the team. We play the game when we blame somebody else for something that has gone wrong. We play the game when we blame external events for how badly things have turned out. We play the game when we blame our job for our lack of freedom. We play the game when we blame our partner for how we feel.

I too have been a very active participant in the blame game. Previously I mentioned how I had wasted 15 years of my life procrastinating about writing a book. For 15 years up until the age of 30, I told everyone that I was going to write a book. But I didn't. I procrastinated and made excuses for not writing.

A big part of that procrastination and excuse making was playing the victim and blaming everyone and everything for my failure to put pen to paper. I blamed my studies at medical school for forcing me to learn a curriculum that was all-consuming. I blamed my job as a junior doctor for not allowing me enough time to do the things I wanted to do outside the hospital. I blamed Hewlett Packard, Dell, and Apple for the exorbitant costs of buying a home computer. I even blamed God for not giving me enough time in the week to do my job, have a social life, go to the gym, even travel somewhere for a much-needed holiday, let alone do some writing.

I was quick to blame others. I was quick to blame my job. I was quick to blame my economic circumstances. But I never blamed myself. It was never my fault. The fault was always something that was outside of me, something beyond my control. I was the victim here. I was the victim of circumstances. I was the victim of other people's needs and wishes. I was the victim of life itself.

At the time, I didn't know that I had slipped into the habit of viewing life through the lens of a victim. I had slipped into the habit of filtering everything that came to my awareness through the distorted perspective of victimisation. So I did what victims do: I refused to take responsibility for what I had done, where I was at, and where I was going. I blamed from morning till night. There wasn't a minute in the day when I wasn't playing the blame game.

When you don't take responsibility for your life, you give that responsibility to someone other than yourself—your parents, your family, your partner, your friend, your boss, your doctor, your teacher. Or you give it to some institution or organisation—your school, your job, the government, the economy. Then you start blaming that other person or institution for how your life has turned out.

Paulo Coelho, bestselling author of many books, including *The Alchemist*,[22] and one of the most influential authors of modern times, said:

> *It's always easy to blame others. You can spend your entire life blaming the world, but your successes or failures are entirely your own.*

Once you're old enough to take the wheel and steer your ship, you're old enough to take responsibility and steer your life to where you want to go. So don't react with blame, which can be instinctive but nonetheless controllable, because that's just taking your hands of the wheel and saying it's not your fault your ship is heading toward the rocks. That's just being a victim.

Rather, be response-able and respond maturely. It's your life. Take the lead in defining who you want to be, determining what you want to do, and designing how to achieve it.

Then take responsibility and do it.

#2: Win First, Learn Second

Successful people learn from their mistakes and failures. They have a different perspective of failure, one that says, "I never lose. I either win, or I learn."

---

[22] *The Alchemist*, Paulo Coelho, HarperSanFrancisco (HarperOne), 1988

As such, there are four rules those in The 5% Club tend to abide by:

1. The Rule of Growth: They constantly improve upon where they went wrong.
2. The Rule of Future Pacing: They imagine themselves winning, of seeing themselves cross the finish line.
3. The Rule of Invention: They use failures as stepping-stones to get where they want to go.
4. The Rule of Perpetual Motion: They keep moving forward and refuse to sit down and stop.

<u>The Rule of Growth</u>

The first rule to never lose, to always win or learn, is the Rule of Growth.

The underlying principle of nature is the continuous advancement of life. Every living thing grows. Every living thing expands. Every living thing progresses forward. Every living thing evolves.

Growth is the nature of life, and the nature of life is growth.

Those in The 5% Club tap into this underlying principle of nature to progress forward. They embrace growth as the natural order of things and avoid resisting it. If they resist, they stagnate, they regress, they decay, they fade away. They know that if they ignore the underlying principle of nature, their dreams will begin to stagnate. Their ideas will fail to progress forward. Their ambitions will decay. Their hopes will fade away.

To avoid this, they embrace the Rule of Growth. They never assume they are the finished product, so they continually ask themselves how they can improve themselves. They know their way isn't necessarily the best and only way, so they are always seeking out ways to improve how they do things. They know they don't have all the answers, so they have the attitude of constantly improving where they went wrong.

They seek to grow. They seek to improve. They seek to evolve. Always.

The Rule of Future Pacing

The second rule to never lose, to always win or learn, is the Rule of Future Pacing.

This is an NLP technique that athletes use in the lead up to a major event, such as the Olympic Games, to improve their chances of winning gold. Athletes will allocate time during their training schedule to visualise their event and see themselves crossing the finish line. In their mind, they perform their event over and over again, seeing and feeling every aspect of the race. If they are a sprinter, they see themselves in the starter's block, they hear the starter saying, "On your marks... get set..." and then they hear the sound of the starter's pistol. They feel their muscles tense as they spring out of the blocks. They hear the roar of the crowd. They smell their sweat. They feel their heart pounding as they race down the track toward the finish line, and then they feel the final lurch as they cross the line ahead of their competitors.

Then, when the Olympics arrive and they're being interviewed, you'll hear them tell the journalist, "I've been preparing for this moment for a long time."

They've prepared their minds and their bodies for success. Deliberately or not, they've actually followed the strategy for success we've been discussing throughout this book, which they've used to channel their inner Nike, the Greek goddess of victory:

> -> 'I Am': They defined and identified who they were—
> an Olympic athlete.

-> 'I Will': They determined their purpose and what they wanted—to participate in the Olympics and win a gold medal.
-> 'I Can': They designed how to do it and planned their destination—they developed a training regime that prepared them for success, including the conviction of winning gold through future pacing the eventual result.

Then they did the next important thing, they took action and did what they needed to do to manifest their success.

So can you.

The Rule of Invention

The third rule to never lose, to always win or learn, is the Rule of Invention.

It's been said that most inventions are just improvements on what's gone before. That's mostly true, but there are some inventions that were completely new in their time and had never been seen before. The wheel is one example. The first aeroplane too. The combustion engine. The atom bomb. The telephone. The radio. The lightbulb. The world wide web.

These are new things that came into existence through the inspiration and dedication of the inventor. As they say, invention is 10% inspiration and 90% perspiration. But imagine if the inventor of the wheel gave up on her first try because the wheel wasn't as perfectly round as she wanted it. Imagine if the Wright brothers gave up after their first attempt and went back to their bicycle shop because it was a lot safer than trying to fly. Imagine if Alexander Graham Bell gave up on his first prototype of the telephone because nobody picked up on the other end.

Inventors have the greatest attitude to failure. They know that failure isn't the end, that it's just something that didn't work. They know that with each failed attempt they are one step closer to succeeding. They know that you only fail when you put down your tools and give up. So they use each failure as a stepping-stone to their future success.

Some, like the great inventor, Thomas Edison, needed 10,000 steps to achieve success. Although he didn't invent the lightbulb, he is credited with perfecting it. But instead of looking at his 10,000 attempts as failures, he preferred to consider them stepping-stones to one of his greatest achievements. He said:

> *I have not failed. I have just found 10,000 ways that do not work.*

Imagine what you could achieve with such perspective?

The Rule of Perpetual Motion

The fourth rule to never lose, to always win or learn, is the Rule of Perpetual Motion.

Similar to the Rule of Growth, which states that the underlying principle of nature is the continuous advancement of life, that growth is the *very nature* of life itself, the Rule of Perpetual Motion states that the underlying principle of the universe is that it is in constant motion.

Since the beginning of the universe, it has always been in motion. It never stops moving. Even if you think you are standing still on the calmest day without a breeze in the air, you are still moving. You might not feel as if you are moving, but the earth is spinning at 460 metres per second, or about 1000 miles per hour. The earth is also orbiting the sun at about 30 kilometres per second (about 66,600 miles per hour). Our solar system in the outer reaches of the Milky Way is rotating around the centre of the galaxy at about 210 kilometres per second (about 468,000 miles per hour). The galaxy itself is moving at 2.1 million kilometres per hour (about

CERTAINTY & KNOWING

1.3 million miles per hour). The universe itself is expanding even faster, and every day it gets faster because it's actually accelerating.

At least in this four-dimensional plane of existence, motion is perpetual, whether you feel it or not. Any appearance of being stationary is only relative, a subjective interpretation based on your relative movement to external objects. On an airplane, once you've reached cruising altitude, it can feel as if you are not moving at all, as though you are seated in a movie cinema. Especially if the lights are dimmed and the windows are shut. It's only when the plane descends or changes direction do you feel you are moving, or when you open the window to have a look at the ground below.

Members of The 5% Club take on board this illusory concept of being stationary. They know that any appearance of not moving forward is an illusion. They know that if they feel stuck, it's an illusion from which they can extract themselves. They don't stay there. They don't stay stuck. They know that if they don't, if they stay mired, they will fail. Which is why they consider complacency a dirty word. So too the concept of being comfortable. So they find ways to get unstuck and keep moving forward.

They embrace Winston Churchill's words of wisdom and run with it:

If you're going through hell, keep going.

They therefore never stop moving. No matter what, they never sit still, they never stagnate. If they don't have a win, they know there's always the next game, there's always another opportunity, there's always something else they can do.

In a way, they embody the philosophy of the shark, of which there are about two dozen species that need to keep moving to stay alive. For these sharks, like great whites, hammerheads, whale sharks, and reef sharks, it is literally a case of swim or die. This is because they need the flow of water through their gills to extract oxygen. If they stop moving, the flow of water stops, the oxygen depletes, and they eventually suffocate. For these sharks, perpetual motion is a matter of life and death.

For those in The 5% Club, perpetual motion is a matter of success or failure.

#3: Be Solution Focused

Do you see a problem in every opportunity, or an opportunity in every problem?

As well as staying focused on your vision and goals, it will also be to your benefit to take on board the perspective of turning problems into opportunities. This means focussing on the result you want, not the problem getting in the way. Embrace the attitude to deliberately and intentionally seek out solutions, because that's the best way to turn a problem into an opportunity.

I used to struggle with this perspective for many years until something happened to cause me to see the nature of problems from a different angle. My daughter joined a new netball club to further her ambitions of playing at a higher level, even state level. This new club, however, didn't seem to rate her ability as a netballer and so they dumped her in the bottom team. Now, I do realise that every father thinks his donkey is a racehorse, but I don't think my evaluation of her abilities was too far outside the truth. I thought it reasonable that she should have been placed in either the top team, or at the very least in the second team. Not the eighth team, where she was now languishing.

After weeks of emails and conversations with coaches and secretaries and decision-makers of the club, my daughter was shuffled up to the fifth team. Not exactly what I was hoping for, but at least it was better than the original decision. Problem solved, or at least I thought.

Not two hours after the club problem had reached a conclusion, my daughter came to me after school and told me that there was

CERTAINTY & KNOWING

now a 'BIG problem' with her school netball team. There were too many girls trialling for the A team and, as she had taken a hit to her confidence with her new club, she was worried she was going to be overlooked.

I threw my hands in the air, thinking, "Will this ever stop?"

At that moment it suddenly dawned on me that problems will never go away. It was foolish to think they would, and it was emotionally and mentally draining to even resist this fact. Problems, I now understood, were here to stay, but so too were solutions. I realised there and then that I could either choose to focus on all the problems that assailed me throughout the day, or I could focus on the solutions that those problems presented. The choice was clear: either embrace the problem or embrace the solution.

I now wake up every morning and say to myself, "Today will be full of problems. But it will also be full of solutions."

#4: Think BIG

There's no such thing as an average person, only an average mindset. Your potential is only limited by your thoughts and beliefs about yourself. Therefore set goals that you see yourself achieving, not goals that you only hope you'll achieve. Think BIG. Think no limits.

They say we overestimate what we can achieve in a day, and underestimate what we can achieve in a lifetime. So set BIG goals that are actually the minimum of what you can achieve, not the maximum limit of your success. Don't set your goals too low. Use BIG goals as steps to your next big thing, not a ceiling that caps a limit to what you are capable of achieving.

Renaissance sculptor and painter, Michelangelo, creator of the masterpiece statue of David and the Sistine Chapel fresco, said:

> *The greatest danger for most of us is not that our aim is too high and we miss it, but that it is too low and we reach it.*

But why should we set big goals and set our aims high?
Because of the person *you will become* in achieving those goals.
If you think little thoughts, your world will be little. If you think big thoughts, your world will be big. So set big goals. Not for the money, not for the possessions, not for the power, not for the fame, not for the material gains. Not for what will come from achieving those goals, but for *what you will become*.

In Constantine Cavafy's beautiful poem, *Ithaca*, he writes that when you set out on your journey to your destination, your Ithaca, pray that the road is long, full of adventure, full of knowledge. But do not expect Ithaca to offer you riches. Her sole reason for existing is to give you the beautiful voyage, to inspire you onward, to arrive at her shores a better person than when you set out.

> *Always keep Ithaca in your mind.*
> *To arrive there is your ultimate goal.*
> *But do not hurry the voyage at all.*
> *It is better to let it last for many years;*
> *And to anchor at the island when you are old,*
> *Rich with all that you have gained along the way,*

The value in setting BIG goals and achieving them is not the value of money or what you earn from the achievement. It's not what you get, but something infinitely more valuable—who you become, rich with all that you have gained along the way.

#5: *Be a Person of Value*

The world owes you as much as you are willing to owe the world.

It's been said that you reap what you sow, which means what you put in, you get out. Put nothing in, get nothing out. Put value in, get value out. Some call it karma, some call it The Law of Reflection. So to fully maximise this law and use it to your advantage, be proactive about it and be a person of value, because the value you put in is the value you get out:

CERTAINTY & KNOWING

Think how to create and add value to this moment, and act with the intention to create and add value to this moment.

In the Game of Life, it's inescapable that what comes around goes around. You can't avoid it. That's just one of the rules of the game. So use it to your advantage and set your intentions on being a maker of value, not a taker of value.

We will go much deeper into adding value to others in our discussion in Part IV on Power Habit #3: Other People Thinking. But for now, again, a good rule of thumb to remember is the 80:20 Rule:

Give 80% of the time, receive 20% of the time.

When you set your intentions on adding value to others 80% of the time, you'll be sure that in the remaining 20% of time, whatever value you have given will be returned to you with interest.

Even if the results don't work exactly as you had intended, you can still rest in the knowledge that your intentions were good and you meant to add value—this alone will fill your mind with a sense of joy, peace, and freedom. This is fulfillment of the highest order.

What, then, does the world owe you?

Will You, or Won't You?

The difference between failure and success can often be measured in the use of one word. People with a habit of failing tend to say, 'I wish...' They wish for something to be different. They wish to be somebody different. They wish they could do something different.

They continually wish for changing circumstances, little realising that circumstances don't change on a wish, they change when the person changes. If they were to consider the five intention statements we have just been discussing, they would be more likely to say, 'I wish I was response-able.' 'I wish I could win first, learn second.' 'I wish I could be solution focused, to think BIG, to be a person of value.'

However, there is greater power in willing something to happen than wishing it to happen. To improve your chances of success, don't wish, rather say, 'I will!'

An important aspect of developing the Power Habit of Self-Assuredness and Self-Belief is to amplify your intent by building unwavering certainty. To help you do this, a powerful exercise is to say, "Yes, I will..." before each of the five intention statements:

1. *Yes, I will* be response-able!
2. *Yes, I will* win first, learn second!
3. *Yes, I will* be solution focused!
4. *Yes, I will* think BIG!
5. *Yes, I will* be a person of value!

Write down these five intention statements on a piece of paper or in a notebook to read and review often, if not daily. Add to these a statement of intent, something that will inspire and motivate you, such as:

- "Yes, I will be response-able! I will not play the blame game. I will take responsibility for my actions and how I feel."
- "Yes, I will win first, learn second! I will not get bogged down in failure. I will use my failures as stepping-stones to my success."
- "Yes, I will be solution focused! I will not be part of the problem. I will be part of the solution."
- "Yes, I will think BIG! I will not think small. I will set big goals so I can grow into the person I am capable of being."

CERTAINTY & KNOWING

- "Yes, I will be a person of value! I will not be a taker of value. I will be a maker of value and use the 80:20 rule of giving and receiving."

Do this often and you watch your self-assuredness and self-belief grow..

CONVICTION: REINFORCING YOUR SELF-BELIEF—I CAN

The final step in developing the Power Habit of Self-Assuredness & Self-Belief is to reinforce your belief in yourself.

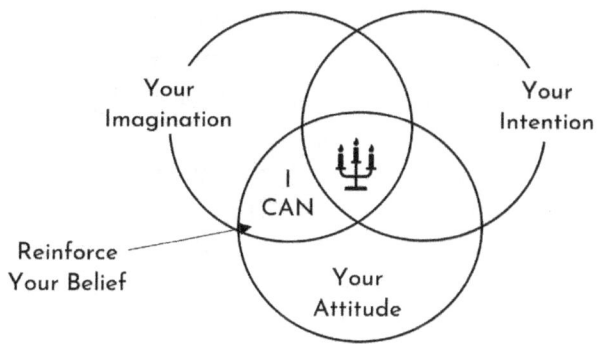

FIGURE 13:   Reinforce Your Belief

Aligning the right Attitude with your Imagination is powerful because it strengthens your belief that you can accomplish all you set out to accomplish. With the right Attitude, you will be willing to do everything that's required to get you over the finishing line.

But where is the finishing line?

That's up to you. It's wherever you decide it should be. The finishing line is the vision of who you want to become and what you want to achieve.

So first set your direction through imagining and visualising the finishing line. Then, like an athlete future pacing her gold-medal victory, imagine yourself crossing the finishing line. Then go out and do what you need to do to cross the finishing line filled with the belief that it will happen.

You need to find that place where the doubts and misgivings about your abilities are dismissed, where the fears of not being good enough and not being deserved enough are unheeded. You need to find that place where negative thoughts are transmuted into golden thoughts, where self-sabotaging beliefs are transformed into self-empowering beliefs.

That place is inside you. It is at the overlap where your Attitude and Imagination align. Here you transcend to the level of knowing you can be and do anything you set your mind to—your 'I Can'.

You might be familiar with the American fairy tale, *The Little Engine That Could*, which has been told in many formats, including films by Disney and Universal Studios. It goes something like this:

> A small red engine is pulling a toy-filled train to a town on the other side of a mountain. The toys are for the children of the town, but the engine breaks down upon reaching the mountain.
>
> A toy clown jumps out of the train and flags down other engines to help them get to the children. First, a shiny yellow passenger engine, then a big black freight locomotive, and finally a rusty old engine.
>
> The shiny passenger engine is too pompous and refuses to help. So too the big freight locomotive, who is too important to bother helping. Even the rusty old engine is too tired and old to help out.
>
> Finally, a little blue locomotive arrives. Although she tells the clown she is only a switcher engine, and has never pulled a train or been over the mountain, she agrees to help them get to the children on the other side.

CERTAINTY & KNOWING

"I think I can," she puffs, and couples herself in front of the toys.

She starts up the mountain, puffing as she goes, "I think I can, I think I can..."

Halfway up, the gradient increases and she struggles with the heavy load, but she continues to puff, "I think I can... I think I can..."

Ever higher she goes, straining with the increasing steepness of the grade. "I think... I can, I think... I can..."

Nearing the top of the mountain, she almost stops, slowing to a crawl, but never giving up, "I... think... I... can, I... think... I... can."

Then, drawing on bravery and hope, she reaches the crest and makes her way to the delighted children below.

"I knew I could! I knew I could! I knew I could!"

Although this is a tale for children on the value of optimism, self-belief, and hard work, it has meaning for adults too.

What would the result have been if the brave little engine said instead, 'Nah, I don't think I can. I'm too little. I'm not strong enough. Surely, some other train is better than me for this job.'

What would the result have been if the brave little engine didn't believe she was of any value to the children? What if she believed she just wasn't any good at being a train engine?

She could have been derailed at any time by her own negative thoughts and fears. But she pushed through. Unfortunately, many of us don't. We get derailed by the negative things we believe about ourselves, we get deflated by the negative words we say to ourselves, so we don't push through.

Here is a calculation on how many negative words the average person says to him or herself in an average year. The calculation is based it on the number of thoughts that psychologists estimate go through a person's mind on a daily basis, coupled with the estimate that, of those thoughts, 80% are negative. The results are staggering:

The average person has 3-17 million negative thoughts per year.

That's astounding. Now let's multiply that by the average lifetime of 80 years: 240-1,360 million negative thoughts per person, per lifetime (and yes, that's 1.36 billion at the top end).

But just imagine the person who has 1.36 billion positive thoughts in their lifetime.

Imagine what they could achieve. Imagine the power of good they could do for others and their community. Imagine the paradise they could create for the world.

Imagine if it were you.

You Can Do It

Here is an exercise that will help you align your Attitude with your Imagination to solidify your conviction, your 'I Can':

1. Identify one or two things in each of your 7 Life Segments that you want to improve or do better: Family & Relationships, Career & Work, Money & Finances, Health & Wellbeing, Learning & Education, Fun & Adventure, Spirituality & Religion (or Morals & Ethics).

2. Next, review the list you've just made and choose your Top Priority Items that you would most like to work on now.

3. Then decide which you will action today and how you will do it.
4. Finally, write down how you plan to achieve your goals over the next 21 days, or however long you feel it will take.

Here are some examples of how to do this exercise:

Family & Relationships:
1. 'I Can' improve and do better: being kinder to everyone, being more helpful with chores around the house, being less judgemental of others, being more loving toward my partner, being more patient with my kids.
2. Priority: being more patient with my kids.
3. Action Plan: I can be more patient with my kids by not being in rush, allowing more time for things to get done, and being more forgiving of mistakes and accidents. I aim to do this every day.

Money & Finances:
1. 'I Can' improve: being better at saving, spending less on impulse, giving more to charity, learning how to invest and make money work for me, paying off my credit card and other debts and loans.
2. Priority: giving more to charity.
3. Action Plan: identify 5 local charities, 5 national charities, and 5 international charities to donate monthly and increase my giving to 10% of my income. I aim to start with my next pay cheque.

Once you identify where you can activate your conviction through Imagination and Attitude, make a written plan to enhance them, and then take action on that plan. You'll find not only that your attitude changes and improves, but you will notice your self-belief changing for the better and your successes begin to mount up.

PART III

POWER HABIT #2

COURAGE & CONFIDENCE

POWER ELEMENT #2

VALOUR

7 THE POWER OF BELIEF

THE MAKING OF ACTION

If the COVID pandemic of 2020-2022 taught us anything, it's that despite our best intentions nothing in life is secure. Security, as it was dramatically shown, is an illusion. Insecurity is the reality.

The pandemic revealed our vulnerabilities on a personal level, relationship level, community level, national level, even global level. It revealed our vulnerabilities on a financial level, healthcare level, employment level, even national security level. Our livelihoods, our careers, our homes, our way of life can quickly and easily be turned upside down. Our sense of who we are, what we do, how we do it, can be suddenly brought into question.

In these moments of vulnerability you need courage. You need courage to face down your insecurities and develop strategies to overcome your problems. You need courage to face your fears and continue to live the best way possible. You especially need a lot of courage during periods of uncertainty when fear and anxiety are just as virulent as COVID-19 itself.

Yet, courage is not out of reach. Courage is not just for the brave, not just for others. Courage is within your grasp. M. Scott Peck was an American psychiatrist who wrote many books, including the bestselling book, *The Road Less Traveled*.[9] In his books, he went into great depths about the human condition, about good and evil, love, values, religion, and spirituality. He also wrote about fear and courage, and he made the remarkable observation that bravery was not fearlessness, not having less fear than anyone else. Rather, he observed, the truly courageous were full of fear, but what separated them from the crowd was their refusal to allow their fear to dictate their actions. He said:

Courage is not the absence of fear; it is the making of action in spite of fear, the moving out against the resistance engendered by fear into the unknown and into the future.

Thankfully, as a human being, you have an abundance of courage. You have the inner power to move out against your fears into the unknown and into the future. Just as humans have always done in every crisis. We have shown courage when we went into lockdown for weeks at a time to stop the spread of the corona virus, not only as individuals but as communities and as nations. We have shown not only courage, but also ingenuity and collaboration, when we galvanised our efforts to hunt down and develop a vaccine for COVID-19 in record time. We have shown courage when we had faith that the worst of the pandemic would eventually pass, that the world would rebuild and renew itself, and that the future still held the promise of joy, hope, love, even peace and freedom.

So, yes, the pandemic reminded us that nothing in life is secure, that insecurity is the 'new normal'. If in fact this 'new normality' is actually new at all, or that it's simply more obvious to us now that we've been forcibly shaken awake to what we thought was real and made to see what is an illusion. But it's also revealed something else, something wonderful and truly marvellous:

Human courage is already there—it's already inside us, as us. It's who we are.

Like happiness, if courage is what you want, you already have what you're looking for. All you need to do is tap into it.

BELIEVING IN YOUR ABILITIES, OUTCOMES & EFFORTS

Confidence is a game-changer for those seeking to be successful and desiring to grow into the person he or she wants to be. Like self-assuredness and self-belief, those who are successful tend to have oodles of confidence. Those with limited success tend not to have it.

The Psychology Dictionary Online[23] defines self-confidence as:

> *An individual's trust in their own abilities, capacities, and judgments, or belief that they can successfully face day-to-day challenges and demands.*

Lack of confidence, by contrast, is the lack of belief in your abilities to get things done. It means you don't believe the outcome will be of any value to you, and you don't think anything you do will make one iota of difference.

Researchers have shown that children with high self-confidence perform better at school and have higher job satisfaction later in middle age. High self-confidence has also shown to improve the chances of survival after serious surgical procedures. Other studies show a strong relationship between self-confidence and achievement or positive mental health. That's why developing and growing your confidence is important to your future success and prosperity.

As we discussed in developing self-assuredness and self-belief, confidence also develops with the clear vision of *who* you are, *what* you want to do, *why* you do it, and *how* you do it. Confidence grows in magnitude with the courage to be the person you want to be. It's hard to be confident without courage, without making action in spite of your fears, yet it's also hard to be courageous without confidence. They are symbiotic.

---

[23] https://dictionary.apa.org/self-confidence

Psychologists identify three main types of confidence:

1. Belief in your *abilities*—the confidence that your skills and abilities will handle most, if not all, future scenarios and find solutions to problems that will enable you to progressively realise your goal.
2. Belief in the *outcome*—the confidence that you will achieve the outcome you plan and prepare for.
3. Belief in your *efforts*—the confidence in the Law of Cause and Effect, that your efforts (causes) will be rewarded with the results (effects) you are working for.

These three types of confidence are strengthened by your three superpowers of Imagination, Intention, and Attitude. If you want to strengthen your belief in your abilities, all you need to do is activate your Imagination superpower. If you want to strengthen your belief in the outcome, all you need to do is activate your Intention superpower. If you want to strengthen your belief in your efforts, all you need to do is activate your Attitude superpower.

It all starts with the right mindset. When you begin to strengthen your beliefs in your abilities, outcomes, and efforts, your courage and confidence will naturally develop and grow. This is important because you will need courage and confidence to take action and do the things you need to do to realise your goals, despite the obstacles, fears, and insecurities that will get in your way. Without courage and confidence, you probably won't take the necessary action. Or if you do, it will be half-hearted and likely to run out of steam before anything meaningful is achieved.

So how do you develop more courage and confidence?

Essentially, it's the same process we discussed in Part II to develop the first Power Habit of Self-Assuredness & Self-Belief:

THE POWER OF BELIEF

-> Awakening your Imagination, Intention, and Attitude superpowers.
-> Getting clarity on your identity of who you are and want to be—I Am.
-> Igniting your motivation—I Will.
-> Tapping into your conviction—I Can.

These three fundamental components—I Am, I Will, I Can—were used to build the Power Element of Faith, which is the faith in who you want to be and what you want to do. These same three components will now be used to build the Power Element of Valour through developing Power Habit #2: Courage & Confidence.

You have the innate ability to do this. Valour isn't just for the heroes of this world. Valour isn't just for the knights in shining armour. Valour isn't just for the servicemen and women who defend our country. Valour isn't just for the police, paramedics, or firemen that serve our community and save our lives. Valour is for the everyday person who is doing the best they can given their situation. Valour is for the everyday person who is trying to improve their life and make this world a better place.

Valour is for the single mum struggling to raise her kids. Valour is for the disabled child going to school every day. Valour is for the unemployed parent trying to put food on the table for the family and keep a roof over their heads. Valour is for the wife who suspects her partner is having an affair. Valour is for those who get up every day, put on their clothes, and continue to do what they do despite life's difficulties. Valour is for the hero in all of us.

Valour is for the hero in you.

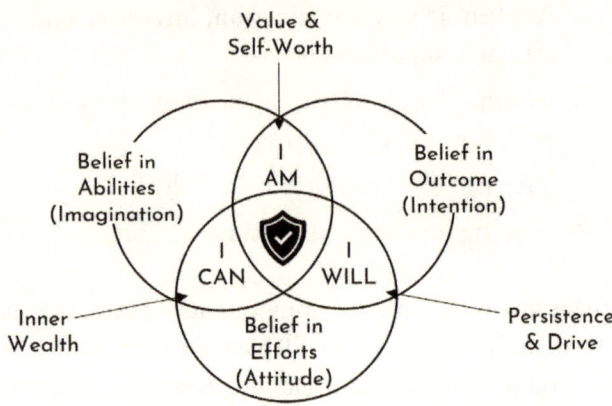

FIGURE 14:   Power Element–Valour

The above diagram explains how your Imagination, Intention, and Attitude align to build the Power Element of Valour:

-> Identity: the overlap where your Imagination and Intention align is where you identify your *value and self-worth*—your 'I Am'.

-> Purpose: the overlap where your Intention and Attitude align is where you maintain your *persistence and drive*—your 'I Will'.

-> Conviction: the overlap where your Attitude and Imagination align is where you expand and grow by investing in your *inner wealth*—your 'I Can'.

The central overlap where the three components of Self-Worth (I Am), Persistence (I Will), and Inner Wealth (I Can) merge and align as one is where the Power Element of Valour is forged.

The Power Habit of Courage & Confidence is how you develop this Power Element. It's how you make your life heroic.

IDENTITY: IDENTIFY YOUR VALUE & SELF-WORTH—I AM

When you know what you want to achieve, you know what you must become in order to achieve it.

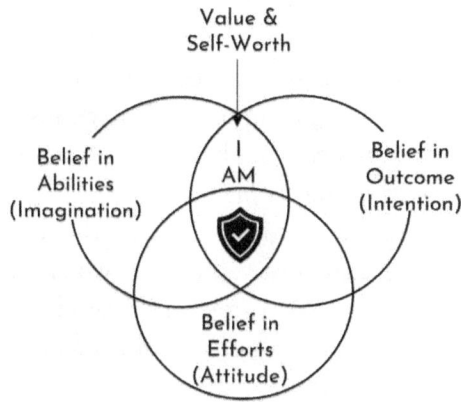

FIGURE 15:   Identify Your Value & Self-Worth–I Am

Want to help find a cure for cancer? Then you'll need to become a doctor or nurse to treat patients with cancer. Or you'll need to become a scientific researcher to organise the studies and examine the data. Or you'll need to become a philanthropist to fund the research.

Want to help eradicate worldwide poverty, hunger, or suffering? Then you'll need to align yourself with a charity like World Vision or Doctors Without Borders. Or you'll need to get involved with international organisations like the World Health Organization and UNICEF.

Or maybe you want to act more locally and support those most vulnerable in your community, like the elderly, disabled, homeless, disadvantaged minorities, abused children. Then you'll need to become a healthcare worker, or social worker, or counsellor, or even a volunteer at your local community or religious centre. You might even consider becoming a lawyer and dedicate yourself to advocating for disadvantaged groups.

You might want to educate underprivileged teenagers, or share the word of God, or deliver babies. Then you'll need to become a teacher, or preacher, or midwife.

Or you might just wish to create works of art that reflect the goodness, truth, and beauty you see in the world, or write an inspirational book, or compose and play music that lifts the emotions of those who hear your lyrics and tunes. Then you'll need to become a painter, writer, or pianist.

Or you might just want to become a mother or father, wife or husband or partner, and create a home in which love, happiness, good memories, and optimism grow and abound like a well-tended garden. Then you must become a person of maturity, wisdom, patience, self-sacrifice, and dedication.

Yet whatever you decide you want to become and want to achieve, identifying your self-worth is integral to how successful you will be. If you don't value your abilities and don't value what you are doing, or even the outcome of what you are doing, then any consequent results will reflect that lack of value. It's again the Law of Cause and Effect at work. If you devalue the cause (who you are and what you do), the effect will be devalued (the results).

The value of the effect is dependent on the value you place upon the cause.

If you don't believe you are capable of achieving anything of value, how you see yourself will reflect that lack of value—you will believe you're not good enough or not clever enough or not rich enough to be successful. If you don't believe the outcome of your endeavours has any intrinsic meaning or worthiness, how you feel about that outcome will reflect that lack of value—you simply won't care what happens, and what you do will be meaningless.

On the other hand, those who have a strong sense of value in who they are as a human being and a strong sense of value of their role tend to attract success. Whoever they are, successful people feel they are valuable. They feel who they are is worthy. Whatever they do, successful people feel it has value. They feel what they do is worthy.

This heightened sense of value and self-worth is something unsuccessful people tend to lack. Rather, they tend to have a shallow sense of self-worth and don't know their true value. Whereas successful people trust themselves and don't rely on others or their circumstances to determine their value or worth, unsuccessful people invariably don't trust themselves and therefore rely on other people and circumstances to determine their perceived value or worth. They have very little self-credibility.

Credibility is a word that will help you identify your value and self-worth. When you give yourself credibility, you are actually giving yourself credit. Credit has a value. It has worth. If you have high credibility, you have high credit. You have high value and worth. If you have low credibility, you have low credit. You have low value and worth.

So finding and identifying your value and self-worth is simply a matter of giving yourself credit.

The Crying Game

In 2004 I was suffering from a severe lack of self-worth and, what I also perceived, a complete lack of credibility. I had just returned to my hometown of Adelaide after 14 years in Sydney, London, and South Africa. I had left Adelaide as a junior doctor and as a single man, and I now returned as an unemployed husband, an unpublished writer, and a father to a young daughter. Over the preceding six years, I had written three fictional manuscripts and received over 250 rejection slips from publishers around the world. The constant rejection from publishers was a constant hit to my self-esteem, which was now at an all-time low. I started to doubt myself as a writer. I started to doubt I would ever get published, and I started to doubt I would ever earn an income from my writing. I had lost belief in my abilities, I had lost belief in my desired outcomes, and I had lost belief that my efforts would be rewarded. My confidence was shattered.

I had left my job as a doctor to embark on a career as a writer, and now I was regretting the decision. To use a poker term, I had gone all in and was now waiting for the river card to determine my fate. Neither my wife nor I had any employment. Our savings had dwindled to almost nothing. We had two suitcases of possessions and a laptop, and that was it. Worse, we were also homeless. We were reliant upon the goodwill of friends and family for food and shelter. To our relief, after a period of housesitting at multiple locations, we managed to find a short-term rental that was fully furnished. We had no furniture, after all, not even a kettle.

Thankfully, my wife found work at a local hospital and some money started to trickle in. I became a stay-at-home dad to look after our one-year-old toddler and to try and do some writing. But write what? My fictional stories were at a dead-end. I was still sending them to agents and publishers, but they kept returning like puppies that nobody wanted. I loved writing fictional stories, and yet I was beginning to feel that non-fiction was where I should focus my efforts. I figured my writing career couldn't get any worse. This crying game wasn't going to get any better soon. What did I have to lose?

The book I had in mind was going to address what I saw as the underlying cause of all the world's problems: hunger, war, rape, disease, poverty, mental health. The cause of our dysfunctional world, as I saw it, was the broken connection with our Source. As a species, we have forgotten who we are, spiritual beings having a human experience. From my point of view, we humans, in the Western World at least, have neglected this fundamental connection to the Source of Life. Some call this God. Some call it

THE POWER OF BELIEF

'The Universe'. Some call it 'Higher Intelligence'. I wasn't, nor am now, hung up on the name of this Source. Maybe it's just 'I Am'. All I knew was that this Source was the Source of All that Is: all Awareness, all Life, all Love. When we lose connection to Source, usually through forgetfulness and the belief that we are isolated and separate from this Source, which is the birth of the ego, that's when fear arises. When fear arises, problems arise. Big problems.

Thankfully, the solution is usually embedded in the problem itself. If the problem is disconnection from the Source, which arouses fear, then the solution is to reconnect with the Source through faith, which is the opposite of fear. If there is darkness, you need light. If there is hopelessness, you need hope. If there is hatred, you need compassion. The problem paves the way for its solution.

But I didn't have the confidence to write about this topic. For a start, I didn't believe a publisher would be interested enough to publish it. Even if it did get published, I didn't believe anyone would be interested enough to read it. I had all but given up on the idea of writing a book on this topic before I had even begun. It just wasn't going to be worth my while.

One morning, as I lay in bed contemplating the pros and cons of writing this particular book, I realised my biggest stumbling block to sitting down at my desk and begin typing was the complete lack of credibility. I had no self-validation. I simply didn't believe I had the authority to write a book that addressed deep spiritual concepts.

"Who do you think you are?" the inner critic kept saying to me. "Nobody knows you. You're a completely anonymous writer. No publisher has ever wanted any of your other books. You're not an expert in anything. Why do you think anybody will be interested in what you have to say?"

I had listened to that little voice day in and day out for the past eight years. It was incessant. It never stopped. Worse, it was utterly convincing. I believed what it said. I was unknown. I wasn't an expert. I had no authority. I had no credibility. I was a fool to think I could even contemplate writing such a book. It was best I forget about the whole thing all together. It was only going to end up like the other manuscripts, rejected time and time again, with no hope of ever being published. Did I really want to put myself through all that pain again?

But that morning I heard another voice. A calmer, quieter, more soothing voice. A voice which reminded me that, for more than a decade, I had spent an enormous amount of time researching evidence to support my beliefs in disconnectedness from the Source. I had examined the writings of the world's main religions, Christianity, Islam, Judaism, Hinduism, Buddhism, even The Tao. I had delved deeply into science, learning and educating myself on the most up-to-date theories and concepts in astrophysics, quantum physics, cosmology, and evolution. I had read philosophical works, ancient and modern, and even brought myself up to speed with the ideas and writings of the New Thought movement. Even though I hadn't received a university degree acknowledging my understanding of the esoteric nature of the universe, I had nonetheless gained quite a substantial knowledge of these deep philosophies and concepts. I had all the credibility I needed.

That inner voice shifted something in my mind. Up until that moment, I realised that I had been waiting for others to give me the credibility to write this book. I had been waiting for others to give me permission. But now I realised I didn't need their permission. I simply had to give myself permission.

Which I did. Once I accepted that I had the credibility to author the book, I gave myself permission to write it. It took another six years, but in 2010 my book, *Your Natural State of Being*,[24] was published.

I had won the only battle that counts—the battle against myself.

---

[24] *Your Natural State of Being: A Pilgrim's Guide*, Scott Zarcinas M.D., DoctorZed Publishing, 2010

The Value of You

When you find your credibility, you feel credible on all levels of being: mental, physical, emotional, and spiritual. You literally feel *incredible*.

Blockages to credibility are therefore blockages to feeling incredible. Blockages come in all shapes and sizes. They are different for everyone. In my case, these blockages to accessing my credibility were literally giving me writer's block. They stopped me from writing for a long time. The belief that I wasn't good enough to write the book because I was an unknown author, I had no expertise, I had been rejected by publishers on numerous occasions, I didn't have anything of interest to say. The list was quite extensive.

Nevertheless, I conquered my credibility issues through the understanding that only I could give myself the credibility I needed. Nobody else could do that for me. Like the Second Tenet of Success, credibility could only come through me, not to me. I had to look myself in the mirror and say, "You are worthy. What you have to say is valid. It has value."

Self-worth therefore comes from validating yourself, which is valuing who you are and valuing what you do. The equation is simple:

Self-Worth = Value of Being + Value of Doing

Any depreciation in your evaluation of who you are as a person and what you do in your day-to-day life will automatically depreciate your sense of validity and self-worth. Any lack of validity and self-worth has direct consequences on your levels of credibility, and therefore your success.

But the strongest sense of validity and self-worth is not built on what you achieve or by your outward successes, it is built on the intrinsic value you place on who you are. Nobody can validate you other than the validation you give yourself. Nobody can give you self-worth other than the self-worth you give yourself. Nobody can give you value other than the value you give yourself.

To seek validity and self-worth through what others value of you is to do yourself a disservice. Others will always find fault in you. Even your partner, even your family, even your best friend. There will always come a time when your value diminishes in their eyes because very few people are capable of unconditional love. How they see you, how they value you, is invariably conditional upon what they get from you. So your value to them will fluctuate over time. Sometimes it will be high, other times it will be low. It won't be consistent.

To depend on others for your sense of validity and self-worth is simply not reliable. At some point, no matter who they are, they will inevitably let you down. Where, then, will you be?

In a hole, probably. Feeling very insecure. Feeling very unloved. Feeling very worthless.

Likewise, your sense of validity and self-worth will be fragile and insecure if it is determined by what title or job description you have. Jobs come and go. Jobs get made redundant. Retirement comes quicker than you ever thought it would. Some jobs have greater social standing than others, but that's not you, that's the job. Once you've retired or taken on a new role, the social standing of your previous employment doesn't move with you, it just gets transferred to the next person to take on that role.

So to invest your sense of validity and self-worth in the job description is to invest in a pyramid scheme; at some point, you'll want to withdraw your investment and there will be nothing there. You'll suddenly realise it's all a scam and you'll feel very foolish.

But you have only scammed yourself. You have made poor investment choices in external people and external situations. The best investment will always be internal, not external. This is where you develop your Imagination, Intention, and Attitude. This is where you have access to your insight, intuition, and inspiration.

THE POWER OF BELIEF

This is where you are connected to the awareness of who you are, and this awareness of self goes wherever you go. This awareness of self is always there no matter who you are with, no matter what job you do, or how many jobs you do. This awareness of self is the only permanent sense you have, the only sense that has been with you 100% of the time, from the day you were born to now.

The best investment, therefore, is internal, to invest in who you are being while you are doing what you do. Your Imagination, Intention, and Attitude are under your control, nobody else's control. So start being valuable to yourself. Start imagining that you are valuable. Start with the intention that you are valuable. Start with the attitude that you are valuable.

Start by saying, "I *am* a person of value. I *will* be a person of value. I *can* be a person of value."

Then you will build your sense of validity and self-worth. Your confidence and courage will grow. You will feel of value to yourself. When you feel of value to yourself, you will be of value to others. When you are of value to others, what you do will be of value to others.

Because value starts with you.

8 THE POWER OF PERSISTENCE

PURPOSE: MAINTAIN YOUR PERSISTENCE & DRIVE—I WILL

THE NEXT COMPONENT of developing the Power Habit of Courage & Confidence and building the Power Element of Valour is to maintain your persistence and drive.

There will always be obstacles on your path. There will always be mountains to climb, deserts to cross, oceans to sail, storms to navigate. These things are inevitable on your journey. Life will always be difficult. You will therefore need to renew your energy stocks along the way. You will need to refuel and keep the momentum moving in the right direction. You will need to keep persisting, keep driving forward, because to stop is to give up and fail.

How you maintain your persistence and drive is by aligning your Intention with your Attitude.

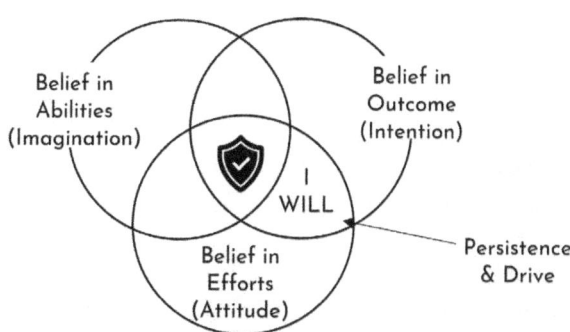

FIGURE 16: Persistence & Drive–I Will

In regard to courage and confidence, this means to align your belief in the *outcome* you want to achieve with the belief in your *efforts* to achieve that outcome. This is best achieved through devotion to a worthy cause—believing in a cause whose outcome fills you with a sense of purpose and to which you willingly dedicate your focus, energy, and effort.

There are therefore just as many worthy causes as there are people on the planet, because each worthy cause is based on your individual and unique service to other people. You will do your best and be successful when you realise you're not an island that's isolated from others and need to do it all by yourself. When you realise we're all interdependent on one another and the best way forward is to support each other, whether in business and work, or in your relationships and family.

Research tells us that having a purpose or cause is beneficial not only to an individual's personal life, but also to the organisation in which they work. When you feel a sense of great purpose in what you do, you feel a deeper commitment to helping others and helping make the world a better place to live. This flows through to helping the organisation that you work for contribute to improving the world and the lives of others. You go to work feeling that what you do really matters.

Space X, the company founded by Elon Musk in 2002, has one of the great mission statements of any company. Their mission is inspiring and, literally, uplifting:

> *To revolutionise space technology, with the ultimate goal of enabling people to live on other planets.*

What a fantastic place to work. Imagine going to work every day knowing that you're helping humanity to become an interplanetary species. How exciting would it be to work in a place that is helping humanity to expand and grow and boldly go where nobody has gone before?

In the past, purpose and meaning were seen mainly as tools to adapt to circumstances. The circumstances determined the purpose. The situation determined the meaning. But Viktor Frankl's book, *A Man's Search for Meaning*,[8] changed how meaning and purpose are viewed. Today, we tend to look at meaning and purpose as motivational drivers to not just cope with circumstances, but to drive toward something beneficial and attainable. In other words,

> *Your purpose determines your circumstances.*

For instance, the value of what you do is directly related to how much you dedicate what you do to the service of others. It's directly related to how much value you create for another, even if it's just one person other than yourself. Like Space X, it's helping the entire planet. But it isn't how many people you serve that determines your value, it is the act of using every moment to create and add value for someone other than yourself.

That's how you build purpose and meaning. That's how you become purposeful, full of purpose, and live a life of happiness and fulfillment. It isn't any more complicated than that:

> *It is the giving of yourself to others—your service—that determines your purpose and value, your success.*

Yet, many people don't do this. They are only interested in serving themselves. For whatever reason—fear, ignorance, shame, greed, vanity—they have not developed the courage or confidence to become anything other than someone who takes direction from their baser instincts. They become slaves to their whims and desires; they become self-serving and thereby live a life of selfishness, greed, addictiveness, neediness, and futility. A life of untapped potential and unmined value. A life not worthy of their talents or indeed themselves.

Which is why it is vital to set yourself a goal to achieve, a port to which you want to sail, a worthy cause to devote your life to. Because without it you are no use to yourself, and if you're no use to yourself you're not going to be of any use to others. You won't be able to serve others to the best of your ability, and you won't find the success or happiness you're looking for.

As David J. Schwartz wrote in his timeless book, *The Magic of Thinking Big*:[25]

> *The individual who fails to set long-range goals will most certainly be just another person lost in life's struggle. Without goals we cannot grow.*

So get your thinking cap on, get a pen and piece of paper, and start writing down what you want to achieve. Start mapping out a route to the destination you want to go to.

And while you're at it, make it worth your while—make it a *worthy* goal. Align your goal with serving others and creating value for them. Make it your cause to which you devote your life.

Then make a start on it.

Your Worthy Cause

The beneficial side-effects of identifying your worthy cause and making a start on it are tangible and intangible. They are both objective and subjective, physical and mental.

The tangible side-effects of striving toward you worthy cause have physical components and actually have positive, measurable effects on your health. Researchers have shown that people who set goals and work towards them have better health outcomes than those who don't:

---

[25] *The Magic of Thinking Big*, David J. Schwartz, Wilshire Book Co., 1959

- They sleep better.
- They have a lower risk of heart problems.
- They have better functioning with aging.
- They even have a 20% lower risk of death.[26]

In fact, those that don't have a worthy cause to which they are striving to achieve, have worse health outcomes and increased vulnerability to boredom, substance abuse, anxiety, and even depression.

Intangible side-effects of having a worthy cause include the resultant happiness, courage and confidence you get from striving toward that worthy goal. Happiness, courage and confidence are intangible because they are purely subjective; only you can experience them. Others may notice your smiling face, or steadfast demeanour, or determined resolve, but only you feel the depths of these feelings.

There are other intangible side-effects too, as listed in the table below:

INTANGIBLE SIDE-EFFECTS	
Happiness and joy.	Courage and confidence.
Inner peace and harmony.	Hope and optimism.
Enthusiasm and excitement.	Lightness of being.
Self-respect and self-worth.	Energy and vitality.
Balance and harmony.	Liberation and freedom.

TABLE 7: Intangible Side-Effects of a Worthy Cause

---

[26] Mount Sinai Medical Center. *"Have a sense of purpose in life? It may protect your heart."* ScienceDaily, 2015

What's more, your worthy cause also gives you a greater sense of meaning and purpose.

Meaning and purpose also have a knock-on effect: they give you drive, determination, perseverance, persistence. With your worthy cause set, you develop a "Never say die!" attitude.

Successful people never give up. Even when all else seems futile, when the whole world seems to be conspiring against them, they keep going. They keep putting one foot ahead of the other, always moving forward, never stopping. They are climbing their mountain and they won't give up until they reach the summit, no matter the cost.

In 2015 I attended a private business conference in Sydney, Australia, and during that conference I met the 64th Australian to successfully climb to the summit of Mt Everest. He was a colleague of the organiser of the event and had been invited to speak to the audience about his experience of climbing the highest mountain on earth, a feat achieved by only 6,000 people (*as of the writing of this book).

He spoke of years of preparation and training to tackle the mountain. Of unbelievable obstacles, freezing conditions and furious winds, of altitude sickness, despair and injury. He spoke of avalanches and seemingly bottomless chasms of ice into which previous climbers had fallen and were never seen again, of tying 3 or 4 ladders end to end and using this makeshift bridge to cross hands and knees to the other side. And he spoke of the final triumph over the mountain.

But it was his depiction of the final moment to reach the summit that I remember most clearly. He talked of the peak of the mountain as taunting the climbers, of making them believe they were closer than they think. Then, just as they thought they were nearing the top, the mountain appeared to move further away. It was as paradoxical as it was soul-destroying: the nearer he got to the peak, the more it seemed to move away.

It was at this moment, just as he was about to reach the peak and realise his dream, that another mountain, the mountain of self-doubt, reared in front of him, seemingly as insurmountable as Everest itself. At this moment, with the freezing air chilling him to the bone, his oxygen supplies running low, all he could do was focus on his feet trudging through the ice, putting one boot ahead of the other.

"I couldn't do anything else," he said, "other than focus on one step at a time."

He could have given up at any point along the climb. But he didn't. He was ultimately successful in conquering Everest, and his story is a great metaphor for the mountains we all set ourselves to climb. Like a marathon, climbing Everest comes down to the simplest, yet one of the most difficult, things we learned to do as a toddler: putting one foot ahead of the other.

There are 4 takeaways from this story of ultimate success:

1. Set yourself a mountain to climb, your Everest—identify your worthy cause.
2. Plan and prepare—you don't just turn up at base camp and start hiking up the mountain; you need to plan how you will conquer your mighty goals.
3. Put one foot ahead of the other—sometimes that's all you can do, but it'll get you to the top.
4. Keep going—maintain and sustain your persistence, even when your goal taunts you and seems to be moving away from you the closer you get.

As Winston Churchill said when he visited Harrow School, his alma mater, in 1941:

> *Never give in, never give in, never, never, never, never—in nothing, great or small, large or petty – never give in except to convictions of honour and good sense. Never yield to force; never yield to the apparently overwhelming might of the enemy.*

In other words, set your course and keep going no matter what.

Climb Your Mountain

Here is an 'I Will' motivation exercise that will help you align your Intention with your Attitude to create purpose and drive:

1. Identify one or two things in each of your 7 Life Segments that you want to achieve: Family & Relationships, Career & Work, Money & Finances, Health & Wellbeing, Learning & Education, Fun & Adventure, Spirituality & Religion (or Morals & Ethics).
2. Next, review the list you've just made and choose your Top Priority Items that you would most like to work on now.
3. Then decide which you will action today and how you will do it.
4. Finally, write down how you plan to achieve your goals over the next 21 days, or however long you feel it will take.

Here are some examples of how to do this exercise:

Learning & Education:

1. 'I Will': learn a musical instrument, learn a new language, learn how to drive, learn how to write a book, learn how to fly a plane, complete my tertiary education, learn how to swim, learn how to code.
2. Priority: learn how to drive.
3. Action Plan: I will learn the rules of the road, book an appointment to sit the learner's test, get my learner's license, book driving lessons, and sit the driving exam to get my license. I aim to achieve this within 12 months.

Fun & Adventure:

1. 'I Will': learn how to surf, join a bowling club, become a member of my favourite sports team, go on an exotic cruise, climb Mt. Kilimanjaro, visit the pyramids of Egypt, attend dancing lessons, go snow skiing with my family.
2. Priority: go snow skiing with my family.
3. Action Plan: ask who in the family would like to go snow skiing, book a week's accommodation in the ski fields, purchase ski passes, organise flights and travel to the ski fields, book ski lessons. I aim to achieve this in the following ski season.

Once you identify what you want to be and do in your 7 Life Segments, make a written plan to achieve your goals, and then take action on that plan. You'll find not only that your motivation lifts and soars, but with it your energy and enthusiasm to achieve all you set out to achieve.

CONVICTION: INVEST IN YOUR INNER WEALTH—I CAN

The next component of developing the Power Habit of Courage & Confidence and building the Power Element of Valour is to invest in what Earl Nightingale regarded as your true inner wealth—your mind, your abilities, your talents, your time.

In his motivational audiotapes on *Insight*, Nightingale said:

> *Our minds, our abilities, our talents, and time represent our true wealth... and it's the investment of our wealth that will determine our rate of return.*

How you invest in your inner wealth is by aligning your Attitude with your Imagination. In regard to courage and confidence, this means to align your belief in your *efforts* to achieve the outcome you want to achieve with the belief in your *abilities* to achieve that outcome. This is best achieved through the investment of your mind, abilities, talents, and time.

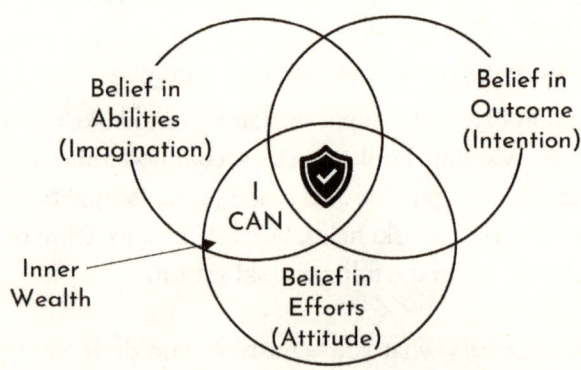

FIGURE 17:   Invest in Your Inner Wealth–I Can

Knowing your inner wealth feeds into your self-belief. The more self-belief you have, the more you believe you can do it. The more you believe you can do it, the more courage and confidence you have to face down any fears and surmount any obstacle along your path to success.

Do you know what assets you already have? Do you know the value of those assets? Are you investing the wealth you already have and maximising your rate of return?

Like any asset, it should work for you not you for it. Money should work for you, you shouldn't work for money. Likewise, your mind, abilities, talents, and time should work for you, you shouldn't work for them.

Growth leads to renewal. Stagnation leads to decay. So if you're not using the assets of your mind, abilities, talents, and time, or you're not investing your innate wealth to progressively realise your worthy cause, your value isn't growing or being renewed.

You're not growing if you're not renewing, and you're not successful if you're not growing.

We've already discussed the asset of time in Chapter 2, so let's do a stocktake of the other assets you have, mind, abilities, and talents, and briefly discuss each in turn.

#1: Your Gold Mind

Are you aware of the gold mine that is your mind? You could, in fact, call it your 'gold mind'.

A version of one of Aesop's Fables, *The Goose that Laid the Golden Egg*, tells of a cottager and his wife who had a goose that laid a golden egg every day. They figured a great nugget of gold must be contained within the goose, and in their greed they decided to kill the goose to get the gold. But to their surprise, they found the goose was no different from their other geese. The foolish cottager and his wife had hoped to become rich all at once, yet all they had managed to do was deprive themselves of the riches they were assured each day if they had remained patient.

This fable about the short-sighted destruction of a valuable resource is a good analogy for the wasted resource of our mind. Like the golden goose, our minds have the ability to produce golden eggs—ideas. Your golden ideas are produced in the factory of your gold mind, which is non-other than your Imagination superpower.

But how often are you using your Imagination to produce golden ideas? What's stopping you? Have you killed the golden goose?

You see, you already have what you're looking for; and when you tap into your gold mine, you'll discover a rich vein of ideas that, when utilised, will help you solve problems and find solutions to achieve your worthy goals.

#2: *Your Abilities and Skillsets*

Are you aware of all your abilities and skillsets? How many of your abilities are dormant and unused?

Recently, a fox decided to pay a visit to my chickens. I have a property on several acres in the hills of Adelaide, South Australia, in which we allow our chickens to roam free-range around the house and garden. Not too far, mind you, because foxes, snakes, and feral cats enjoy the company of chickens too.

On the day the fox came, one of the chickens learned a skill it didn't know it had—it could fly. When the fox charged out of the bushes, the frightened chickens sprinted in all directions as if their life depended on it. It did.

The fox took a liking to one particular chicken and sprinted for it across the grass in a blur of orange. The chicken, barely managing to keep ahead of the fox's snapping jaws, suddenly came to the end of the garden where it abruptly dropped in a steep slope to the bottom of the hill. With nowhere to go, it did the only thing it could: it took off into the vacant airspace like a F/A-18 Hornet taking off from an aircraft carrier. And stricken with fear, it kept flapping and flying as if it were the most natural thing for a chicken to do.

It flew 60 metres down the hill to a pine tree, where it took refuge from the fox and waited for me to collect it and bring it back to the safety of the coop. The fox went to its den hungry that evening.

When I reflected on that incident, it occurred to me that humans are not too unlike chickens—we don't use our innate skills and abilities until we absolutely have to. Sometimes, we don't even know we have those skills and abilities, and it takes a frightening or life-threatening incident to realise what we can actually do.

As the prolific American author, Jodi Picault, wrote in her book, *My Sister's Keeper*:[27]

Maybe who we are isn't so much about what we do, but rather what we are capable of when we least expect it.

But why wait for such extreme measures to reveal your hidden abilities?

You already have what you're looking for, and when you ask it will be given to you; when you seek, you will find.

When you knock, the door will be opened to you.

#3: Your Talents and Gifts

Your talent is the gift you were born with.

But for a great many of us, being 'gifted' is not something we believe we are. We usually associate a gift or incredible talent to others. Usually it's something we consider the reserve of famous actors, writers, or sportspeople. It's not something we normally attribute to ourselves.

---

[27] *My Sister's Keeper*, Jodi Picault, Atria Books, 2004

Every mother knows that her baby is born with a personality. No two babies come into this world, even from the same mother, with identical personalities. That personality is then moulded in the kiln of everyday experiences of childhood and teenage years, and later refined in adulthood.

Talents are like personalities—they come as part of the package when you enter into this world. Everyone is born with a talent, something they are naturally good at. A talent, though, is just a natural ability to learn a specific skill in a shorter period of time compared with the average length of time it would take to learn that skill. A talent is just a natural ability to learn a skill faster than others. Not better than others, just faster.

Here are some talents and gifts that you might identify with:

- The gift of storytelling or playing a musical instrument.
- Understanding numbers or languages.
- A natural talent for sport.
- A talent for acting, dancing or writing.
- Technical or scientific talents.
- The gift of empathy and understanding.
- Creative talents.
- Seeing patterns in nature.

The list of talents is long and varied. Your talents, though, are more than just the result of good genes. They are also not the result of what you have learned through your schooling and environment. Talents transcend genetics and location.

When nurtured with intent and effort, they grow into strong skillsets which can, over time, be mastered.

PART IV

POWER HABIT #3

OTHER PEOPLE THINKING

POWER ELEMENT #3

VALUE

9 THE POWER OF SERVICE

THINK VALUE

IF I WERE to ask you to list the top five most successful people you know or have heard of, who would they be? What are their most striking features?

I'm guessing they would have, in varying degrees, so-called 'status of success':

1. *Money*—they'd be rich and have financial freedom at the very minimum.
2. *Fame*—they'd be famous and, if not celebrity or sporting household names, they'd be easily identified in the streets, on the news, on social media, or in the print media.
3. *Power*—they'd hold positions of power in government, financial institutions, corporations, religious, and even sports organisations.

These are the symbols that most of society would deem as being successful or having 'made it'. But what of character? The accomplishment of great character is far more difficult than making money. Anyone can make money over a lifetime. So is a person of upstanding integrity, generosity, kindness, persistence, self-sacrifice, patience, and resilience not also successful?

Consider again the top five successful people you identified and whether or not they are also persons of character. Now consider whether you know others who don't have as much money, fame, or power, and are probably not seen as 'successful' by society's standards but are nonetheless persons of character. They may be poor, relatively unknown and even invisible to the rest of society, and they probably don't wield power of any measurable sort, but they are persons of value. When discussing the virtues of success, it was Einstein who put it this way:

> *Try not to be a man of success, but rather try to be a man of value.*

Einstein knew that being a person of value is how you get membership to The 5% Club. Your value to others is the key that gets you through the door of success, and one of the best ways to be of value is to develop the attitude of what leadership expert, John C. Maxwell, calls, 'Other People Thinking'.

> *To be a person of success, think and be of value to others.*

In other words, think what other people would like and be of value. Think what other people want. Of course, what you would like and what you want is important. But don't just think about what you would like. Don't just think about what you want. Your value comes from thinking about others. Your success comes from Other People Thinking.

Remember, your goal is to be valuable. Value to others is the key to attracting the success and happiness you are looking for. The parable of the *Teacher and the Balloons* explains this concept of adding value through Other People Thinking in a simple and concise way. It goes like this:

> One day, a teacher handed a balloon to each of her students and asked them to blow it up and write their name on it. Then she instructed the students to toss their balloon into the hall.

With the hall filled with balloons, the teacher moved through the hall to mix them all up. Then she instructed the students to find the balloon with their name on it. After five minutes of frantic searching, no-one had found their personalised balloon.

The teacher then asked the students to take the balloon nearest to them and hand it to the person whose name was on it. In less than two minutes, every student was holding their personally signed balloon.

The teacher spoke to the students. "These balloons are like happiness. You probably won't find it when you're only searching for your own. But if you care about someone else's happiness, it will ultimately help you find your own."

CHANGE YOURSELF, CHANGE YOUR WORLD

By now, you are getting the picture of how to build your Power Habits of Success by using the mantra-like affirmations of 'I Am! I Will! I Can!'

Repeating these affirmations—I Am! I Will! I Can!—in the laboratory of your mind embeds them into the DNA of your thoughts, emotions, and behaviours. The more you do it, the longer you do it, the bigger and broader your Power Habits become. They become you, and you become them. You become a success first in your mind and inner world, which are the intangible rewards of success we've discussed previously, like joy, peace, freedom, harmony. Then follows material and outer world success, the tangible rewards of money, relationships, career, possessions, and so forth. That's how the Game of Life works:

First, be a success inside, then success will follow outside.

Only by changing your inner world will your outer world change. It has to be this way. The Law of Cause and Effect means it can't be any other way—your inner world is the cause, and your outer world is the effect.

I remember vividly as a junior doctor in London, UK, when this law played out in my own circumstances to great effect. I was late for the morning ward round yet again. I had slept in, resenting to have to get up early and commute for over an hour to get to the hospital by 8am. Frustrated and annoyed, clutching my stethoscope to my chest as I ran down the long corridor to the paediatric ward, I said to myself, "God, I hate this job. Why does the job have to be like this? Why can't it change?"

Then a voice inside my head made me stop in my tracks. I literally stopped mid-stride in the middle of the corridor, struck motionless as if I'd just ran into an invisible wall. The voice had said, "Scott, the job isn't going to change. It's always going to be the same job. Only you can change."

This was the first time that I had truly realised that it was my own *attitude* that was causing all my frustration and irritation. My attitude was causing my misery. I had thought it was the job, the external situation, that was the cause of all my problems. It wasn't. It was me. My attitude was first cause, and my experience of the world was the direct effect of that cause.

In order for my world and my life to change, I had to change first. Jim Rohn, motivational speaker and bestselling author of *The Keys to Success*,[28] spoke about an inspirational teacher he had as a young boy. That teacher told Jim Rohn that if he would change, then everything else would change for him.

The teacher said, "If you will get better, then everything will get better for you... If you change your philosophy, you will change your habits. If you will refine your thinking, if you will change and accept some new disciplines, if you will turn the corner where

---

[28] *The Keys to Success*, Jim Rohn, Brolga Publishing, 2002

you've been in the past, go for a new life in the future, all kinds of remarkable things will happen for you, *if you will change."*

Before he met his teacher, Jim Rohn said that at the age of 25 he used to hope that things would change. He hoped that the government would change. That the tax structure would change. That his boss would change and pay him more money. That economics would change and prices would come down. That circumstances would get better.

But then he realised that those things were always going to continue. They would always be the same. He realised that all those things that happened to him, to all of us, were kind of like the wind that blows. But he also realised that if you just let the wind blow, it wouldn't take him where he wanted to go. He therefore needed to use the wind to take him to the dreams he had, to the equities he wanted, to the money he wanted, to the income he wanted, and to all the things he wanted his life to have. He realised that he couldn't leave his future just to the wind, just to the economy, just to the structure of the way things were happening around him. He realised that he had to learn to set a good sail.

That's what he learned from his teacher. That the wind was going to blow how it was going to blow. Politics was always going to be politics. The economy was always going to be the economy. And however it turned out was the way it was going to be. He therefore needed to learn not to wish for a better wind, but to wish for the wisdom and the skills and the learning so that he could set a better sail.

So Jim Rohn went to work. But he didn't go to work to try and change the economy. He didn't go to work to try and change the community. He didn't go to work to try and change the government. He didn't go to work to try and change his boss or his company. He didn't go to work to try and change his circumstances. Instead, he went to work to try and change himself.

All he had to do was work harder. Not on his job. Not on his boss. Not on his company. But on *himself*. If he improved, then his life situation would improve. He didn't have to change anything going on outside him, that was just the wind blowing. All he had to do was change what was going on inside him.

That's how Jim Rohn's life changed. That's how things started working for him. It's also the same lesson I learned scampering down the hospital corridor late for work. I had to change my attitude to life before life changed for me. That's why Gandhi said we should be the change we wish to see in the world. Change, even global change, begins in our inner world.

Over two decades have passed since that early morning wake-up call, but the memory and the effects of that insight are still as relevant to me today as back then. The lesson is simply the lesson of cause and effect, which I will repeat because it's so important:

Your inner world is the cause. Your outer world is the effect.

Your inner world sets into motion what the outer world will reflect back to you. What you put in, you get out. But the Law of Cause and Effect also works to your benefit. It all depends on how much of yourself you put into this moment. Put in a little amount of wood on the fire, get out a little bit of heat. Put in a lot of wood on the fire, get out a lot of heat.

Sounds obvious, but you will only get a return on what you invest. But first you must invest. You must first put money into your savings account before the bank can pay you any interest. The only interest paid on nothing is nothing.

But how many of us want a return on no investment? How many of us want to see the money first before we'll invest? How many of us want something for nothing?

Yet that's not how The Law of Cause and Effect works. It requires a cause for there to be, in its proper place and turn, an effect. Which is just that: a *return* of what you first put in. Like a boomerang, the law demands a cause in order for the effect to come back to you.

In other words, you can only receive what you first give.

By this law, the hand that sows is the hand that reaps the harvest. The harvest doesn't come first; it requires seeds to be sowed. The harvest returns to us the seeds that have been planted. For was it not said 2000 years ago, "As ye sow, so shall ye reap"?

You've got to give before you can get. The quickest, most instantaneous way you can begin to use the Law of Cause and Effect to your advantage and have it work for you, not against you, is to shift your mindset and embrace the attitude of first investing (giving), then receiving (getting).

> *Know, believe, and trust that you must first give unto others before the world can give unto you.*

It is the spark that ignites the flame, and that spark is your mental attitude toward Life. Life waits for you to give it what it needs to return the favour. Like starting your car engine, Life cannot mobilise and propel you forward without you first putting the key in the ignition. Remember, it is *our attitude to Life that determines Life's attitude to us.*

Got a poor attitude? Always want something for nothing? Not prepared to do more than you absolutely have to?

Then Life will reflect your inner world back to you. Your external return will be in direct proportion to your inner attitude, and you will probably not be given membership to The 5% Club.

Got a good attitude? Always willing to put the effort in? Always prepared to do more than what you're asked to do?

Then Life will reflect your inner world back to you. Your external return will be in direct proportion to your inner attitude, and you will most likely be given admission to The 5% Club, if you are not already a Life Member.

When you gain membership to The 5% Club and are welcomed through the doors into the community of success, the first thing you will notice is the attitude of all those who are there. They don't have a "What's in it for me?" attitude. They don't have a scarcity mindset, of competing for every morsel of food like a junkyard dog, of believing that it's every man, woman, and child for themselves.

They have a "What can I do for you?" attitude. They have an abundance mindset, of creating more of what's good for everyone, of wanting success for every man, woman, and child. Because success for others is their success.

Truly successful people have an attitude of Other People Thinking.

That's because the most successful people in life are those who have worked out the most important aspect of success: *how to serve others to the best of their abilities.*

THE VALUE OF SERVICE

When asked what he thought the purpose of life was, Einstein replied, "To serve others."

Are you at that place yet? Are you thinking like a truly successful person? Do you have the attitude that will get you membership to The 5% Club?

Most people don't. They want the effect before they put in the cause. They want to get before they give. They want to arrive at their destination before they leave.

But remember you must first think like a successful person (cause) before the world reflects success back to you (effect). It isn't difficult, but like my younger self running down the hospital corridor late for the ward round, it does require a subtle change of mindset. Your world isn't going to change until you do.

THE POWER OF SERVICE

Your world isn't going to change until you develop Other People Thinking.

Therefore, as the successful person you want and intend to be, there are three main conditions of Other People Thinking that you will need to be mindful of and seek to develop:

1. Your *role and purpose* toward others.
2. Your *intention and attitude* toward others.
3. Your *actions and behaviours* toward others.

Developing and maintaining Other People Thinking is essential if your intent is to be more successful and impactful. You are not an island. Everything you have is because other people were involved in giving you what you now have, and they will be needed now and in the future to get what you want and become the person you want to be. You can't do it alone. You can't do *anything* alone.

Just think of the food you'll eat for dinner. The vegetables were grown by a farmer. The meat was processed in an abattoir. The bread was baked by a baker. You probably purchased the food from a supermarket, grocer, or butcher, or it was delivered to you. You used a car or public transport to get to the supermarket, which required roads and petrol and electricity that had to be built by somebody.

The point is, we are all interdependent on other people. We need other people for the things we have, and other people need us for the service we give or the products we help make. Every community, every town, every city in the world relies on other people. To think otherwise or to believe you've done everything yourself is false and can only accentuate your failure and limit your membership to The 5% Club.

Which is why developing Other People Thinking is the third Power Habit. In Part II and III, you began developing the first two Power Habits of Self-Assuredness & Self-Belief, and Courage & Confidence, using this formula:

THE POWER OF YOU!

-> Awakening your Imagination, Intention, and Attitude superpowers.

-> Getting clarity on your identity of who you are and want to be—I Am.

-> Igniting your motivation—I Will.

-> Tapping into your conviction—I Can.

These three fundamental components—I Am, I Will, I Can—have been used to build the Power Elements of Faith and Valour. These same three components will now be used to build the Power Element of Value, which you will need to utilise throughout your journey of success.

What may surprise you is that you are already a person on value. We confirmed this in our previous discussion on developing self-worth. You are therefore already halfway to being the successful person you want to be. You just need to activate your value by cashing in your own cheque, so to speak.

So if success and happiness is what you want, you already have what you're looking for. All you need to do is tap into your own inner value and self-worth by developing Other People Thinking.

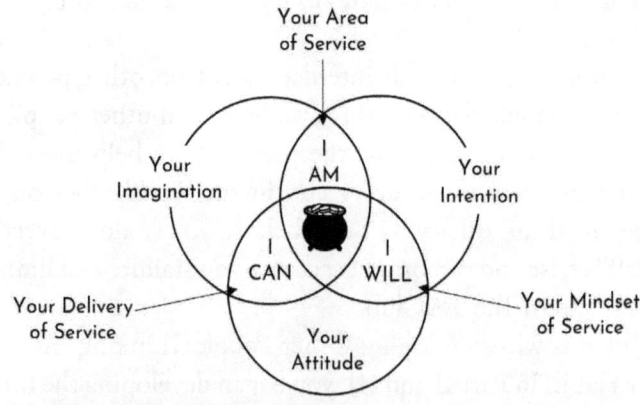

FIGURE 18: Power Element–Value

The above diagram explains how your Imagination, Intention, and Attitude align to build your value:

- -> Identity: the overlap where your Imagination and Intention align is where you identify your role in your *area of service*—your 'I Am'.
- -> Purpose: the overlap where your Intention and Attitude align is where you develop your *mindset of service*—your 'I Will'.
- -> Conviction: the overlap where your Attitude and Imagination align is where you add value through your *delivery of service*—your 'I Can'.

The value of who you want to be and what you want to do is in the central overlap where the three components of your Area of Service (I Am), Mindset of Service (I Will), and Delivery of Service (I Can) merge and align as one Power Element called Value.

The Power Habit of Other People Thinking is how you develop this Power Element. It's how you make your life valuable.

IDENTITY: IDENTIFY YOUR AREA OF SERVICE—I AM

You may have heard of the term, Unique Selling Proposition, or USP. The marketers and salespeople of the world constantly strive to identify and hone their USP. They work on the notion that they have to somehow stand out from the crowd to make consistent sales, to be successful. They believe their business has to be unique in some way or another. If not, another business will attract the attention of the customer. Hence their efforts to establish their USP.

Really successful people have also identified their USP, but it's the opposite of what the marketers and salespeople would understand: they have a Unique *Service* Proposition. They think other people. They think service.

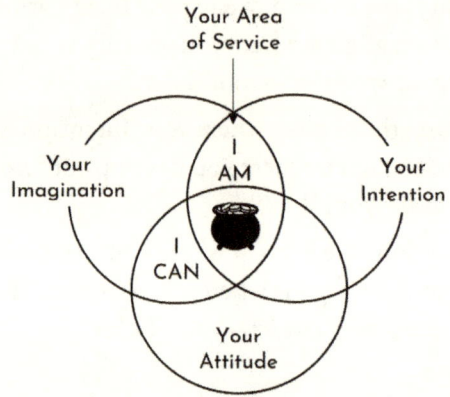

FIGURE 19:   Your Area of Service–I Am

The most successful shopkeeper is not the one who is grumpy and unsmiling when you walk into his shop. He is the one with USP and serves his customers with delight and courtesy.

The most successful waitress is not the one who is disdainful of her patrons and quick to temper. She is the one with USP and serves each person with a cheer and a smile.

The most successful taxi driver is not the one who is impatient and angry with the traffic on the roads. He is the one with USP and serves his passengers with patience and calmness.

The most successful doctor is not the one who is disrespectful and patronising to her patients. She is the one with USP and serves her patients with care and consideration.

The most successful people in the community share this one commonality: they are devoted to serving others. In whatever field of work or endeavour they're involved with, the service of others is their Number One priority. They are makers, not takers. They make every moment and every situation bigger by serving and adding value to others. They don't take from each moment or try to suck it dry, they don't try to squeeze everything they can out of the situation or the person they're dealing with.

They are donors, not leeches. They know their investment in other people will pay off. They know that Life richly rewards those who invest as much of themselves as they possibly can into the moment, and this 'investment' is primarily achieved through the act of service.

That's Other People Thinking. That's USP. That's success.

Finding Your USP

To serve others is ultimately an act of self-service. This is because it is inclusive, not exclusive. When you help others to grow, to build, to expand, you find that, quite remarkably, you too grow, build, and expand. So when you help and serve others, you are also helping and serving yourself. Investment in others is an investment in yourself.

But should you only focus on yourself, should you only serve yourself, the opposite happens. Serving yourself to the exclusion of others ultimately works against you because the intention is to exclude, to separate, to isolate, to withhold, to have power over others. Inclusion, by nature, is to increase. Exclusion, by nature, is to decrease. The effect of which is to retard your growth, to minimise, to shrink, to stagnate.

Recall what Einstein said, that our purpose in life is to serve others. Those who are fortunate to live more than a few decades on this planet get to fulfill many roles: child, sibling, student, partner, parent, leader, worker, boss, manager, healer, carer, friend, colleague, team member, and many, many other roles. Each role offers the opportunity for Other People Thinking and to be of service

So the question everyone should ask themselves is, "What's my role in this life? What's my purpose for being here?"

In each of your 7 Life Segments you have at least one role, often multiple. For instance, in Family & Relationships, you may have the role of mother, wife, friend, grandmother, sister, and other roles. In Learning & Education, you may have the role of student in an educational institution, or you may be embarking on a training course for personal pleasure. You may even take on the role of a teacher and educator, mentor, coach, trainer, or facilitator in professional or personal settings.

In Money & Finances, you may be the breadwinner in your family, or you may be the one who looks after the bookkeeping and bank accounts, stocks and shares or other investments. You may even take on the responsibilities of being the landlord of your rental property.

Some roles last longer than others. Some are brief and last only for a day, a week, or a month at a time, like a coach or tutor, while other roles can last for years and even a lifetime, like a sister or brother. So now that you can identify the many roles you play during your lifetime, you can now start to focus on your areas of service and your USP.

Here's a task you can do to help with this. Take a piece of paper and a pen and consider these questions:

1. What is my main or most important area of service in each of my 7 Life Segments?
2. What are the areas of service that I'm already good at? What's my USP?
3. What are the areas of service that most need my attention?
4. How can I improve these areas of service?
5. What is the one thing I can do today and for the rest of the week that will have the most impact on my ability to serve others?

Here are some examples of how to do this exercise:

Money & Finance:
1. My main areas of service are: earning income for the family; organising the weekly and monthly household budget; paying the bills; grocery shopping; saving for holidays; investing for retirement.
2. The area of service I am already good at: organising the weekly and monthly household budget.
3. The areas of service that most need my attention are: investing for retirement.
4. I can improve this area of service by: booking an appointment with a financial advisor and developing a financial retirement plan.
5. The one thing I can do today and for the rest of the week that will have most impact on my ability to serve is: stop procrastinating and book the appointment with the financial advisor.

Health & Wellbeing:
1. My main areas of service are: buying the weekly groceries/food for the family; being responsible for the family's medicine supplies; organising the doctor's appointments; cooking healthy dinners; packing the kids' lunch boxes for school; driving the kids to sport practice and matches.
2. The area of service I am already good at: driving the kids to sport practice and matches.
3. The areas of service that most need my attention are: cooking healthy dinners.

4. I can improve this area of service by: cooking meals with more vegetables and less meat, oils, butter, and sugar.
5. The one thing I can do today and for the rest of the week that will have most impact on my ability to serve is: plan healthier meals for the family.

Once you identify your roles and area of service in your 7 Life Segments, make a written plan to achieve your goals, and then take action on that plan. You'll find not only that your enjoyment of service will lift, but with it your relationships to others will improve and become less of a chore.

10 THE GOLDEN RULE

PURPOSE: DEVELOPING YOUR MINDSET OF SERVICE—I WILL

THE NEXT COMPONENT of developing the Power Habit of Other People Thinking and building the Power Element of Value is to develop your mindset of service.

When you serve others, you add value to their lives. It's as simple as that.

But just because you serve someone, it doesn't mean that you are their servant. Service is not servitude. You are not a slave bound to a master because you serve. You are free to serve as you choose, not as others choose you to serve.

How you develop the mindset of service is by aligning your Intention with your Attitude. In regard to adding value to others, this means to align your intention to serve with the attitude of The Golden Rule, of doing unto others as you would have them do unto you. The value of your service is best achieved through free will—the freedom to decide who you serve, why you serve, and how you serve.

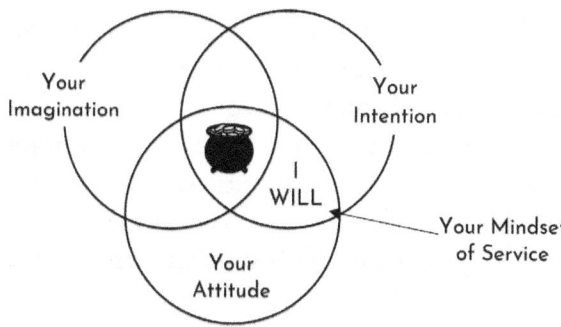

FIGURE 20: Your Mindset of Service–I Will

It is your free will to decide on what service you give, which is why, again, your attitude of service should always be front of mind. Always be thinking, "How can I make this moment bigger? How can I help? What do others need right now that I can give?"

It isn't always money. In fact, it is rarely money that other people need from you. Many other things take precedence. Here are six ideas to remember to help focus your mindset on how to serve others. They are easy to remember because together they create the sentence: I SERVE!

> I: Importance
> S: Smile
> E: Empathy
> R: Recognition
> V: Value
> E: Educate

Let's examine these now.

I: Importance

Who is the most important person on the planet?

You, of course. Everyone thinks this way. Everyone thinks they are the most important person on the planet, and that's the way it should be. Everyone should value themself and their self-worth as vitally important and equal to others.

Next time you meet someone, whether it's an old friend, a customer, your mother, or you're meeting them for the first time, remember that they consider themselves to be the most important person on the planet. So treat them that way. Treat each person as though they were the most important person in the world, because to them *they are*.

Listening is one of the easiest and best ways to show someone that they are important to you. Not listening to them is an easy way to show them that they are not important to you.

I recall a social event that I was looking forward to attending because I knew an old colleague was going to be there, someone I hadn't seen for quite a while. I was excited to catch up on old times and have a few drinks and a yarn. Unfortunately, the experience didn't turn out as I had hoped. Within about ten seconds of chatting, my old colleague seemed to lose all interest in the conversation. I guess because it wasn't about him. He kept glancing at his watch, shifting from foot to foot, looking over my shoulder, and had an expression that said he was genuinely disinterested in anything I had to say. Needless to say, I didn't feel very important to him.

Most people just want to be heard. When they feel heard, when they feel understood, they feel important. So the simple act of listening is a powerful way to convey to someone that they are someone of importance to you. You don't even have to say anything, just listen. You don't need to fix anything, just hear what they have to say. That's often all you need to do. We have two ears and one mouth, as they say, so we should listen twice as much as we speak.

You can treat others well by listening well. Serve them well. And watch how you are treated in return.

You'll be pleasantly surprised.

S: Smile

Sometimes a smile is all someone needs. A smile can be a ray of sunshine for someone under a heavy cloud.

In my early days as a junior doctor I was a pretty grumpy fellow, as you might have guessed. I didn't smile a lot. In fact, I more or less had a permanent frown etched into my forehead. I didn't want to be at the hospital most days. I wanted to be elsewhere, travelling the world, visiting friends, going out to pubs and clubs, writing my books, seeing my girlfriend. Worse, the hours were horrendous.

Starting at 8am, I would often not walk into my front door until 7 or 8pm. Then there were nightshifts, which came around all too often and all too quickly. Then there were the weekend hours. Some weekends I would arrive at the hospital at 8am on a Saturday and then spend the next 50 hours or so on call in the hospital, not arriving home until the Monday evening. This also often without any sleep.

Sure, it wasn't all doom and gloom. There were good days too. There were good people I met, and good people I worked with. But the bad days far outnumbered the good days. To say I felt trapped is an understatement. When you're not passionate about your career, when you feel forced to do the work, when the hours are long, when you're perpetually sleep deprived, and when the pay cannot even cover a mortgage, you can understand the frustration.

Still, it was my decision to do the job. I made the choice to become a doctor. I made the choice to look for employment in the hospital system. I made the choice to keep doing it. Which probably made it worse, knowing that I was completely responsible for the situation I was in. Hence the permanent frown.

Yet, despite the bad moods, there was a glimmer of light. This glimmer of light took the form of one of the janitors. Every time I saw him, in total contrast to my permanent frown, he had a permanent smile. Whether I was racing down the corridor late for another ward round, or I was dashing to the emergency department, or I was rushing to the delivery theatre, there he was. Always smiling. Always jovial. Cleaning the floors with a permanent smile on his face.

One day, again in a rush to attend a ward round I was late for, I hurried past him, barely noticing what he was doing, barely noticing the patients and other staff in the corridor.

"Mornin' Doc!" he said, a beaming smile on his face.

For some reason, I stopped. Even though I was late, and I knew I was going to get in trouble with my boss, again, I stopped and

THE GOLDEN RULE

looked at this fellow. Really looked at him for the first time. He had a round, Asian face, with deep olive skin, and he seemed to be a good head shorter than me. I figured he was approaching 50 years of age, so at least twenty years my senior. He was holding a mop and smiling as broad and as wide as the Cheshire Cat.

I looked at him, thinking, here I am, a doctor, who has a tertiary education in medicine and science, and here was a fellow without any higher education yet had a deeper understanding about life than I could currently comprehend. I was intrigued.

You know something I don't, I thought. "Good morning," I replied, and smiled back, then hurried down the corridor to my ward round.

Of the thousands of doctors, nurses, physiotherapists, allied health workers, and admin staff that I have worked with, this janitor is the one who I remember the most. I never found out his name. I never found out where he was from. All I know is that he brought a ray of light into my life when I needed it most.

You too can help shift the mood of someone simply with a smile. Emotions are contagious, and there is science behind this. Your brain has a type of neurone called 'mirror neurones'. They exist in birds, primates, and humans. One way a mirror neurone works is to mimic the actions, moods, and behaviours in others. This means that when you see sad people, your mirror neurones 'fire' and mimic the sadness you see, causing your mood to dip and feel sad. You 'buy into' their sadness and feel sad.

When you see angry people behaving with aggression, your mirror neurones 'fire' and mimic the anger and aggression you see, causing your emotions to become hot and angry too. You 'buy into' their anger and become angry.

The same happens when you see happy people smiling and hear them laughing. Your mirror neurones 'fire' and mimic the happiness you see and hear, causing you to smile and feel happier. You 'buy into' their happiness and feel happy.

This is why laughter is infectious. When you hear people laughing, your facial muscles twitch in response and a smile begins to form on your face. Soon you're laughing with them.

So serve others with a smile whenever you can and make the moment bigger and better and lighter.

E: Empathy

This is the ability to understand and share the feelings of someone else. It's the ability to put yourself in their place as if you were them, to 'walk in their shoes', and offer guidance or help should it be appropriate.

Empathy isn't sympathy, which is to feel sorry for someone, or even pity, and psychologists have identified five types: Cognitive, Emotional, Compassionate, Somatic, Spiritual. We will discuss each briefly now.

Cognitive:
This type of empathy is considered 'personal perspective', which is putting yourself in someone else's place and seeing the situation with their *perspective*. It is a rational, thoughtful, logical, reasoning, understanding empathy rather than an emotional empathy.

Emotional:
This type of empathy is considered 'personal distress', and involves an emotional response like the mirroring we discussed in *S: Smile*. There is a 'contagion' aspect to this type of empathy, when we 'catch' the mood of the other person and is emotion-based rather than reason-based.

Compassionate:
This type of empathy is considered 'personal concern', and involves the concern for another's situation with the added behavioural aspect of taking action to help them find a resolution to their

problem or issue. Compassionate empathy is considered the most appropriate type of empathy.

Somatic:
This type of empathy is considered 'personal pain' because it involves actually feeling someone else's pain as a physical symptom. You might even say, "I feel your pain!" when you witness a friend or colleague suffer a mishap, like twisting their ankle or hitting their head against a low ceiling. You might even wince and blurt out, "Ouch!"

Spiritual:
This type of empathy is considered 'personal enlightenment' and most closely resembles Buddhist 'detachment', whereby you are able to see the world and the events unfolding around you from a 3rd person perspective without the investment of personal emotion, desires, needs, and ego. It's to see the world and others like a movie on the big screen in front of you.

So understand your best type of empathy that best suits your personality and the next time you encounter someone who is in need of empathy, serve them a big dish of it and help them to digest their problems in a way that they can find resolution.

R: Recognition
One of the most basic, fundamental human needs is to be recognised and acknowledged. To recognise is to re-cognise, to re-know. In *Your Natural State of Being*,[23] I devote the whole book to the five most basic human needs: joy, security, acceptance, peace, and freedom. Essentially, you can pare these needs to one thing: *love*. We all want to love and to be loved.

Paradoxically, it's also why we crave more money, power, and possessions. Money, we believe, will buy us happiness. Power will give us the freedom to do what we want. Possessions will make us wanted and desired by others, and make us feel good about ourselves and our achievements. Possessions will validate us. That's why we chase after these things, so that we can feel happier, safer, wanted, at peace, and free. We'll be more lovable.

But probably the greatest need of all is the need to feel accepted by others. We all need to feel worthy and respected. We all want to belong.

One way to look at this is inclusion versus exclusion. When others welcome us into their group or tribe or family, we feel a sense of inclusion and acceptance. We feel we're 'one of them'. But to be excluded is to suffer.

I recall the pain of my young daughter one day after school when she came home in tears because her friends had excluded her from their group. As it turned out, it was over a misunderstanding, as is most often the case, but her pain was real and raw and emotional. She had been rejected and she felt unworthy and humiliated.

School kids are always excluding one another. It's part of the powerplay of friendships that we all experience at one time or another. But it reflects our innate human need to belong and to be accepted by our peers. As Brené Brown puts it in her book, *The Gifts of Imperfection*:[29]

> *A deep sense of love and belonging is an irreducible need of all women, men, and children. We are biologically, cognitively, physically, and spiritually wired to love, to be loved, and to belong. When those needs are not met, we don't function as we were meant to. We break. We fall apart. We numb. We ache. We hurt others. We get sick… the absence of love and belonging will always lead to suffering.*

---

[29] *The Gifts of Imperfection: Let Go of Who You Think You're Supposed to Be and Embrace Who You Are*, Brené Brown, Hazelden, 2010

It is a human need to be needed. It is a human desire to be desired. It is a human want to be wanted. We crave acceptance and belonging, and when it isn't forthcoming it leads to personal suffering.

So give the greatest gift you can to someone: *Recognition*. Re-*cognise* them. Re-*know* them. Welcome them. Embrace them. Serve recognition as often as you can, as much as you can, for as long as you can, and watch how you improve the lives of others.

Then watch how your own recognition, respect, and self-worth improves with them.

V: Value

Every moment is an opportunity to serve others and add value.

Leadership expert, John C. Maxwell, says that the most important attribute of a leader is the intention to add value to others. Whether you're a leader in your own business, in a team, in a club, a school, or in your family, the consistent attitude of adding value to other people is what will determine your level of influence as a leader, without which nobody will listen to you or follow you.

As Theodore Roosevelt said,

> *People don't care how much you know until they know how much you care.*

It's how much you care as a leader that will determine your effectiveness as a leader.

It's interesting that research into employment trends show that most people resign and leave their job not because of the work, but because of the boss. Most people seem to like the work they do, but their work becomes intolerable because of their boss or manager.

This has been true in my own experience. As a junior doctor, despite my own personal misgivings about my career, I frequently sought employment elsewhere because I couldn't relate to the consultants that I worked under. I recall one hospital where I had very little, if any, respect for the consultants in my department because of their 'me first' attitude and the dismal way they treated their underlings. They were slave drivers, looking after their own self-interests first and did not seem to care about their junior staff at all. I very much felt like a number, cannon fodder to throw into the war zone that was the emergency department.

When I looked at my bosses, I shook my head and said to myself, "I do NOT want to be like you... or you... or you... or you... or you!"

There was not one single boss I looked up to and wanted to emulate. They didn't care about me, and, if I'm honest, I didn't care about them. I'm not even sure they cared about their patients. I had to leave.

So the lesson I'm painting is this:

> *You will have no influence whatsoever until you care about the people you want to influence.*

You will not be respected by others until you care about the people you interact with and have relationships with, both personally and professionally.

And one of the best ways to show people how much you care about them is to continually add value to their lives. Find out what they need and give it to them.

When you add value, you serve. When you serve, you add value.

E: *Educate*

Education is the path to knowledge, and it has long been recognised as the most reliable asset to lift individuals, communities, and even countries out of the cycle of poverty. Education is key to wealth, whether it be personal wealth or national wealth. Any nation that suppresses the education of its people, either totally or targeted toward a particular segment of its population, such as females, or a racial sect, tend to be poorer than those more liberal countries that strive to educate all its population irrespective of sex, race, religion, or political affiliation.

Education is vitally important. Knowledge gained through education is important. But it has to be the right knowledge. It has to be the right education. Otherwise, whatever education and knowledge has been gained won't find practical application. Without practical application, it won't benefit the individual, and if it won't benefit the individual it won't benefit anyone else, it won't benefit society.

So the best kind of education is that which has practical application for the individual, for others, and for society. An education that has practical application is usually that which fulfills a need. Knowledge that has practical application is usually that which finds a solution to a problem. The word here is progress. Education and knowledge must help individuals and society progress. Ultimately, it must help humanity progress.

It must also do this at the expense of no-one. Right education, true knowledge, comes at no cost to anybody. Nobody should gain knowledge, or use that knowledge, to the detriment of others. To paraphrase Wallace D. Wattles, American New Thought author of *The Science of Getting Rich*,[30] the purpose of true knowledge is the advancement of all at the expense of none.

Knowledge is empowering. As the saying goes:

> *Give a man a fish, you feed him for a day; teach a man how to fish, you feed him for a lifetime.*

That's powerful. When you can educate someone to the extent that they become self-determined, you've empowered them for the rest of their life. When you educate someone in the techniques to better understand themselves—who they are, what they can do, why they're here, how they can achieve—you help them become

---

[30] *The Science of Getting Rich*, Wallace D. Wattles, Elizabeth Towne Company, 1910

the person they are capable of being. You help them activate and maximise their potential.

You help them to live a fulfilled and valued life.

CONVICTION: ADDING VALUE THROUGH YOUR SERVICE—I CAN

The next component of developing the Power Habit of Other People Thinking and building the Power Element of Value is to add value through the delivery of your service. Once you have identified your role of service and developed the right mindset of service, the next step is to follow through on your service and actively deliver it.

How you deliver your service is by aligning your Attitude with your Imagination. In regard to Other People Thinking, this means to align your attitude to serve with innovative and imaginative ways to serve. This is best achieved through the implementation of The Golden Rule, to do unto others as you would have them do unto you.

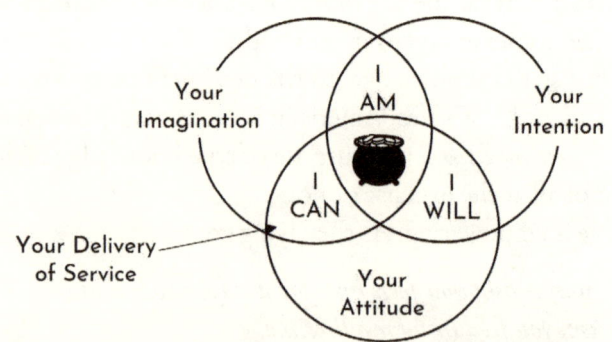

FIGURE 21:   Your Delivery of Service–I Can

We've repeatedly emphasised the importance of having the right attitude, because attitude, as we know, is the magic word. Your attitude is the wand from which magic happens. Get your attitude right, and your world is right.

THE GOLDEN RULE

But how does this apply in your practical, day-to-day life?

Let's use the attitude of safety as an example. A ship's captain and a pilot of a passenger aircraft share the same attitude and intention of 'safety first'. To the captain and the pilot, safety for their passengers and crew is paramount. They are single-mindedly focussed on safety. Everything they do is with the aim of arriving at their destination safely.

Because of this attitude, they don't take unnecessary risks. They follow protocols and guidelines. They have manifests and checklists. All their thoughts and actions are focused on getting their passengers, crew and cargo safely to port.

Imagine, though, if upon boarding your cruise ship you overheard the captain boasting how fast he could get to the next port through a section of reef that other captains were too scared to sail through? What if you glimpsed the pilot in the cockpit taking a swig from his hipflask before telling the crew to get ready to take off?

You wouldn't feel very safe, would you? That's because you know the captain and the pilot are not thinking 'safety first'. They don't have the right attitude to be in control of the vessel on which you've just boarded.

Whatever your job, whatever your role in life, your attitude sets the tone of your experience because it determines the focus of your thoughts, which in turn determines the focus of your actions. You have probably experienced this in moments when you are rushed. If you are late for an important meeting, your attitude is: "I have to get there as quickly as possible or I'll get in trouble."

So you speed through the traffic, maybe shoot through a couple of amber lights, cut people off, swear at a few bicyclists that slow you down, and pray that you don't zip past a police car or speed camera and get a speeding fine. Then you rush into the meeting only to realise you've forgotten your briefcase.

In this situation, your attitude is one of speed, not of safety.

You need to get to your destination as quickly as you can. So your actions and behaviour reflect that attitude. Hopefully you don't have an accident on the way and you avoid hitting a pedestrian or bicyclist.

Parents of newborn babies know how important safety is. On the first trip home from the hospital, the baby is carefully restrained in a capsule, which itself is secured in the backseat of the car by the seatbelt and safety hook. The parents then tentatively reverse out of the car park and slowly make their way home, keeping well below the speed limit and ensuring a huge distance between them and the car in front should they suddenly have to slam on the brakes. Then they breathe a huge sigh of relief when they pull into the driveway and turn off the ignition.

In this situation, the new parents are terrified of having an accident and are on high alert. Their sole thoughts are for the safety of the baby, and so it should be.

In the scenarios of rushing for your meeting and getting your newborn baby home safely, your attitude determines your behaviour. When you think speed, you act in a rush. When you think safety, you act calmly.

When you have the right attitude, you have the right behaviour.

This is true of every person and every profession. You are happy to send your kids to class because you know the teacher has the best interests of her children at heart. You keep returning to your family doctor because you know she has your health and wellbeing in mind. You eat at your favourite restaurant or diner because you know the chef keeps a clean kitchen and uses only the freshest ingredients.

You reward others who have a great attitude, and this you usually do with your money and your patronage. You trust them to serve you well and you develop continuing relationships with them. They reward you with valued service, and you reward them with the appropriate payment.

The people who add value to you and your family are the people you reward. The same is true for yourself:

Be of value to others, and they will reward you in kind.

There are many ways to be rewarded, not just with money. You can be rewarded with being trusted, by friendship, by being considered a person of integrity, and by being held in high esteem. You can be rewarded by being given more responsibility at work or in your family environment. You can be rewarded by being included in organisational or sporting teams, in decision-making, in big projects. You can be rewarded by simply being appreciated, by being welcomed, by being thanked.

The Golden Rule

A consistent, good attitude reaps consistent, good rewards, which is why your attitude is vital in determining your levels of success. Talent and ability can only take you so far. Determination will take you further. But it's your attitude that will determine how far you go and how successful you become.

One of the best attitudes you can have is the attitude of service. But it also needs to be put into practice. Your service has to be practical. It has to be actioned. It has to be delivered for it to be of value to someone else.

Consider the exercise at the end of the previous chapter and the answer you gave to the one thing you can do today and for the rest of the week that will have the most impact on your ability to serve others. The next step after identifying this area of service is to motivate yourself into action. You might have the best-laid plans of mice and men, but plans remain wishes without action. You need to turn your wish into will, and a great motivator for action is The Golden Rule:

Do unto others as you would have them do unto you.

In other words, do for others as you would like them to do for you. The opposite is to do unto others before they do unto you. To take from others before they can take from you. To shoot first and ask questions later. To jump into the lifeboat before all the women and children. To advance yourself at the expense of others.

In your personal and family life, in your career or business, any short-term gain at the expense of another will not last in the long term. The Law of Karma ensures all things are eventually evened out. What you throw out to the universe boomerangs back. The quality of energy you give to others is reflected back to you sooner or later. You can't run away from it because you can't run away from yourself.

What is returned to you may not be in the same form as what you sent out, but it will have the same impact. For instance, if you commit adultery, the negative actions of cheating on your partner will suffer a negative reaction, usually in the form of guilt or paranoia. Despite the pleasure of being with someone else, you will know it's wrong and hurtful and you will feel guilty about what you have done. You may dismiss the initial guilt by justifying your actions, convincing yourself that your partner isn't a good partner, that you and your partner have drifted apart, or that your partner just doesn't understand you anymore. But the guilt will still be there.

Or you will be racked with paranoia, hoping your partner never finds out what you've been doing, hiding your mobile phone from them so they can't read your secret text messages, panicking when you realise you've left it in the bedroom on the charger. Or you've forgotten to change the password on your email account so your partner can't accidentally find out your deceit.

Negative behaviours have returned to you as negative emotions.

THE GOLDEN RULE

If in business you cheat on a deal, or you treat your customers as fools, or have little concern for the welfare of your staff, this too will return to you. For instance, if you agreed to pay a contractor for the work he has done for you, but then deliberately stall on the payments knowing that it will be more expensive for him to involve the lawyers to get his money back, then whatever financial gain you've made will be met with future pain. You might justify this as 'fair business', or that you have to protect your own finances, but in the end you know it's wrong. You will avoid looking at yourself in the mirror. You might even start to feel physical discomfort, palpitations in the chest, queasiness in the stomach, headaches in the morning. Something will happen as a repercussion of the negative energy that you have discharged to the universe.

If you pay forward negative energy, it will eventually be paid forward to you in the form of a payback.

In 2019 I bought a second-hand car that turned out to be more trouble than it was worth. I needed a car urgently because my old car had a terminal gearbox problem that was going to cost more to fix than what the car was worth. So it was sent to the car graveyard, leaving me in a spot of bother.

I went to a car dealer, test drove a couple of vehicles, and decided on a make and model that I thought was reputable. Before I committed to buying, I searched the internet for reviews of this make and model, thinking I was doing my due diligence. The reviews were all positive and agreeable, the car itself had only done 60,000 kilometres, so I signed on the dotted line, organised the finance, and drove home in my new car. Then the problems began.

The coolant began leaking. The air conditioner didn't quite do its job. The brakes needed replacing. They tyres were worn. Worse, it was burning oil. I queried the oil burn with the car dealer, who told me that it was well within 'tolerated limits'. Little did I know, this particular make and model was renowned for burning oil, and that the head company had been taken to court years earlier and ordered to fix the issue. The engine had a design fault, which caused the piston rings to go floppy at certain temperatures and allow oil to be sucked up into the spark plugs. The company had recalled hundreds of thousands of vehicles around the world to fix the problematic piston rings. But not my car.

For some reason, the previous owner didn't have the engine rings replaced. Instead, she sold the car to the car dealer and passed on her problem to someone else. Ultimately, me. By the time I discovered what the issue was, my car was burning a litre of oil every 200 kilometres. I used to joke that my car had a 2-stroke lawnmower engine.

I took the car back to the car dealer who said it was not their problem. The warranty had expired, so all I could do was go to the original company and ask them to fix it. This I did, without any luck. The company said they were no longer liable for the issues of this make and model, but if I wanted to pay A$10,000 they would fix it for me.

I said thanks but no thanks. I continued to drive the vehicle for another couple of years, topping up the oil with every fuel tank and replacing the burnt out sparkplugs every 5,000 kilometres. Then the engine exploded.

I was travelling to the beach with my daughter, heading up the freeway when the power suddenly dropped and the engine gave way. I called a tow truck and had the car towed to the mechanic, who told me that the second and fourth pistons had melted and were unfixable. The car needed a new engine. This would cost A$14,000.

Buyer beware, they say. I can certainly vouch for that. But the takeaway lesson for me was a lesson in The Golden Rule. Neither the original owner nor the car dealer followed this rule. They were only interested in shipping their problem to someone else, and to do it as quickly as possible.

I myself could have passed this problem on and got rid of an irksome issue, but I knew that would only be inviting more trouble in the future. I knew that if I sold the car with a dodgy engine to somebody else, I'd feel guilty and remorseful. I knew that every time I saw the car drive past me, I'd feel shame. I didn't want to give someone else my problem, and I didn't want to feel guilty or shame. I especially didn't want the bad karma.

So I made the decision to fix the problem and not pass it on to anyone else. I could now quite happily sell this car or trade it in knowing that it has a brand-new engine and that I won't be paying forward any problems, at least to my knowledge.

I do wonder, though, what karma the original owner and the car dealer are suffering today.

Practical Ways to Serve Others

The Golden Rule is therefore an antidote to bad karma. When you pay forward good energy, good stuff comes back. Not always in the form of money, or possessions, or career opportunities, but it can do. More often than not it's in the form of positive emotions, like joy, fulfillment, goodness, peace, reassurance, wellbeing, self-love.

Act, then, in a way that you would like others to act and behave toward you. Think and speak in a way that you would like others to think and speak toward you. Listen and care in a way that you would like others to listen and care toward you. Give and forgive in a way that you would like others to give and forgive toward you.

This is how you serve in a practical way. This is how you add value in a practical way. The below table is a list of practical ways you can serve and add value to others:

PRACTICAL WAYS TO SERVE OTHERS		
Do the right thing.	Be patient and kind.	Be tolerant.
Donate to charity.	Volunteer your time.	Smile often.
Give praise.	Be thankful.	Lend a hand.
Teach with wisdom.	Forgive often.	Turn the other cheek.
Be curious.	Don't judge.	Listen with empathy.
Give generously.	Love unconditionally.	Be welcoming.

TABLE 8: Practical Ways to Serve Others

So, a good way to develop practical ways of service is to activate your Imagination and think of ways you can use the Golden Rule to serve others in practical ways. A good practice is to frequently ask yourself:

What would others like in this situation?

PART V

POWER HABIT #4

PLANNING, PREPARATION & PERSEVERANCE

POWER ELEMENT #4

COMMITMENT

11 THE POWER OF COMMITMENT

THE POWER OF PLANNING

IF YOU FAIL to plan, you plan to fail, as the business coaches of the world like to say.

This is a truism which is not just relevant for business success, but also for your own personal and professional success. Planning for success, though, is just a roadmap. It isn't the journey, as no roadmap could ever be, but the right roadmap will guide the way to who you want to be and where you want to go.

Yet to arrive at that place you want to be, you need to know your destination in advance (what you want), and then work out the pathway to reach that destination. With a good roadmap, you can even anticipate obstacles and difficulties along your journey and plan your route accordingly.

Going on a road trip is a great analogy for your journey through life, and one of the best and most scenic road trips I've ever taken is the drive from Denver, Colorado, to Las Vegas, Nevada. In the mid-90s, I rented a Mustang and hit the road with a friend I'd met along my travels through the USA. It was springtime in the Northern Hemisphere, and the weather was perfect. Without a cloud in the sky and no threat of rain or snow, we drove over the snow-capped Rocky Mountains via Aspen and descended into the Nevada desert. On either side of the highway, huge mesas and giant cacti dominated the landscape, reminding me of classic cowboy scenes from all the old John Wayne westerns.

Then, 10 to 11 hours later, as the evening dimmed and we approached the sparkling lights of Las Vegas, the massive disc of the moon lifted above the desert horizon and I could almost hear Dean Martin crooning from the tumbleweeds, "When the moon hits your eye like a big pizza pie... That's amore!"

We pulled into our hotel on The Strip, tired from the long drive but eager to hit the bars and casinos and have fun. The day had been a success. We knew what we had wanted to achieve and had arrived safely at our destination.

So, the point about planning is this:

Why, when we would never spend 8 to 9 hours in a car or bus or train not knowing where we were going, do many of us spend 80 to 90 years of our life not knowing where we want to go?

A lot of people resist planning, especially the carefree and young, because they fear it will take away the spontaneity and fun of life. Yet, my travelling buddy and I had plenty of spontaneous moments during our road trip to Las Vegas. We'd had fun pulling over to the side of the road for scenic photos of the mountains or desert, having leisurely meal breaks, and chatting with locals at the roadside diners.

Planning, then, just sets the route. What you do along the journey is up to you.

In one of my early fiction books, *Samantha Honeycomb*,[31] I originally included a scene where Samantha encountered a free-spirited dragonfly called Derek. He was a cool, surfer-dude, drifting on the wind without a care in the world, happy to go wherever the breeze took him. Derek ended all his sentences in 'man' or 'yeah, man', and I kind of had a soft spot for him, but my editor killed him off. With a stroke of her pen, she eliminated him as ruthlessly as any flyswatter.

---

[31] *Samantha Honeycomb: A Pilgrim's Chronicle*, Scott Zarcinas, DoctorZed Publishing, 2006

"He isn't necessary to the story," she wrote in blood-red ink at the side of my manuscript.

I was slightly put out, and slightly more devastated at losing a favourite character, but I understood my editor's reasoning and accepted Derek's premature demise. Although I did secretly resurrect him in a brief scene when the main character, Samantha, noticed a dragonfly hovering above the sunflowers on her journey through the Crazy Lands. This encounter causes her to ponder the difference between his life, drifting from moment to moment without any goals or aims, and her intense desire to reach her goal, Beebylon, the magical hive where honey dripped from the walls and dreams came alive.

The underlying message I was trying to convey with Samantha's encounter with Derek the Dragonfly (may he rest in peace), was that drifting through life without a destination to reach or a plan on how to get there probably kills spontaneity more ruthlessly than any editor or strategic planning will. Drifting from job to job, partner to partner, town to town, might seem like a bohemian and spontaneous lifestyle, but it is more reactive than bohemian, more stifling than spontaneous. It might be fun for a while, but if your life becomes a pinball ricocheting from bumper to bumper, you're more likely to get tired and worn out than achieving any significant success you want for yourself.

Success requires commitment to a plan.

THE POWER OF PREPARATION

Planning and goal setting is essential if you want to achieve even a modicum of success during this lifetime, and just as essential to becoming the person you want to be. But there's also something else to add to the discussion, and that's to acknowledge that preparation is just as vital as planning.

To expand the 'failing to plan' adage:

If you fail to prepare for success, you successfully prepare for failure.

Preparation is not just another word for planning. Preparation differs both in nature and in definition, and there are two main types of preparation we need to consider:

1. Constructive Preparation: Preparing what you need to succeed (e.g. skills, education, tools of the trade, practice).
2. Receptive Preparation: Preparing for the results in advance (e.g. expectancy, belief, active faith, future pacing).

Recall what the Roman philosopher, Seneca, said about success, that luck is what happens when preparation meets opportunity. Successful people may seem lucky at first glance, or they may have luck attributed to their success. But, if luck has anything to do with it, it's because successful people have made their own luck.

On the surface it might appear that success comes easy to some than it does to others, or they seem to have a golden touch, but that's because we haven't seen the thousands of hours of practice and hard work that successful people have put in while nobody was looking. We just see the accomplishment and think it's easy for them. We haven't seen their preparation for success.

So an important habit of success is to actively position yourself—prepare—for when an opportunity comes your way. Otherwise, if you're not ready for it, if you're ill-prepared, if you're out of position, the opportunity will be missed.

Let's discuss the two types of preparation in more detail.

THE POWER OF COMMITMENT

#1: Constructive Preparation—Preparing What You Need to Succeed

Like saving money for a holiday or for investing in property or the stock market. Or getting the education you need for a particular job or career, or developing the skills that you know will be required on the job.

If your dream house comes up for sale but you haven't saved the deposit required to get the mortgage you need, then the opportunity will slip by.

I illustrated this point to my youngest daughter leading up to Christmas 2020. It was less than five weeks until the big day and she wanted to buy an iPhone for her elder sister. We searched the internet for an available iPhone that matched what her sister would want, and settled on a second-hand model for A$500. The problem was, she had only saved $60 in her piggy bank.

All throughout the year, my wife and I had encouraged her to save her money for when an opportunity came that she would need it. Unfortunately, she didn't take our advice, claiming she didn't know what she wanted to save for. When the time came to look for Christmas presents, however, and she didn't have the money saved for what she wanted to buy, the message started to sink in.

I could see she felt sad that she couldn't buy the present for her sister, so I loaned her the money on the agreement that it would be paid back in three months (which would be another life lesson for her that I want her to learn: don't borrow what you can't pay back), but for the time being I wanted to teach her a valuable lesson in constructive preparation:

> *Putting aside some money for unknown or unseen future opportunities puts you in a favourable position to capitalise on those opportunities when they arise.*

The same applies with your dream job. Every job has a barrier of entry, some higher than others, and in a free and egalitarian society that's usually based on levels of education. If you want to be a lawyer, you need to go to law school and get the proper legal education. If you want to work in a trade as a plumber or electrician, you need to first complete an apprenticeship.

As a general rule, you won't be able to sidestep the barrier of entry and access the opportunity to be a lawyer until you have a law degree. You won't be able to access the opportunity to be a plumber or electrician without first completing the apprenticeship. Without educating yourself and developing the required skills, the opportunity will remain out of reach and inaccessible to you.

But it doesn't stop there. Education is just the beginning, just the foot in the door. Preparing to achieve real success in your chosen career also means thousands of hours of honing your craft. There's no escaping it. That's what this type of constructive preparation, and ultimately your success, requires.

They say overnight success takes 20 years, and speaking coaches will advise you to do 10,000 hours of presentations in front of a live audience before you can become any good at professional speaking. Piano teachers say the same thing about playing the piano: you won't be a proficient pianist without practicing for 10,000 hours or more.

It's what's known in professional circles as 'The 10,000 Hour Rule'. This rule has quantitative and qualitative requirements. The quantitative requirements are the 10,000 hours, the physical effort and the time required, such as practicing and honing your skills. It basically means that whatever you do a lot of, you generally become good at it.

Greg Norman, Australia's most famous and successful golfer, would practice for hours before any tournament, hitting thousands of golf balls on the driving range before even thinking of stepping foot onto the first tee. He practiced relentlessly. He took the time to hone his craft. So when the opportunity came, he was prepared, and he won many tournaments. He made his own luck.

In his heyday at Manchester United, David Beckham would stay behind when all the other players had left the training field and practice his trademark 'bend it like Beckham' free kicks at goal. He practiced relentlessly. He took the time to hone his craft. So when the opportunity came during game time, he was prepared, and he won many games for Manchester United and many trophies. He made his own luck.

In contrast, the qualitative requirements of The 10,000 Hour Rule are mainly attitudinal, in respect to your attitude toward your effort and your attitude toward improvement. Your 10,000 hours will have a greater impact if you have the attitude of wanting to improve all the time and get better, and not just maintain the status quo.

In my high school days, one of my cricket coaches used to say over and over again,

> *It isn't practice that makes perfect; it's the perfect practice that makes perfect.*

He would emphasise that there was no point in practicing badly or practicing the wrong technique; that wouldn't improve your game. Only the perfect practice will improve your game, and that meant having the right attitude to begin with.

Up until I'd heard those words, I had treated practice as a chore, something I had to do to keep my spot in the school team. I enjoyed batting and bowling, but not fielding, especially at practice. I wasn't the best fielder on the team to begin with, and my attitude toward catching and throwing and diving was pretty lacklustre, which showed on the field during matches. Looking to keep damage to a minimum, our team captain often banished me far out of harm's way down on the boundary where it was least likely for the ball to be hit to and where the team could be sheltered from too many of my mistakes.

I hadn't yet learned that the only disability in life is a negative attitude, as the winner or 23 Paralympic swimming medals, Jessica Long, said. The penny only dropped when I joined a cricket club and expectations and competition for places were higher. I was expected to not only be a good batter and bowler, but a good fielder as well. I had to compete with many other players to make the team, which meant a change in attitude toward fielding. So I began to implement the mantra of the 'perfect practice makes perfect' and, by the end of the season, my fielding had improved so much I was considered one of the better fielders on my new team.

The 10,000 Hour Rule is both quantitative and qualitative, and you can apply it to any career or any sport or any activity you choose. The question is: Have you applied it to yours?

#2: Receptive Preparation—Preparing for the Rewards of Success

The second type of preparation is receptive, which is essentially the mental *expectancy* of future success.

First, you plan your roadmap to achieve what you set out to do. Then you upskill and educate yourself on what you need to do and hone your craft, and then you prepare for the successful achievement of it. As international speaker and bestselling author, Brian Tracy, puts it:

> *Decide what you want, and then act as if it were impossible to fail.*

Receptive preparation means you actively prepare to receive the rewards and success you have planned for before they have arrived, or before you arrive at the destination you have planned to arrive at. You vividly envision you'll have in your hands what you set out to get, which includes the emotions and feelings you'll experience upon achieving your desired outcome, and then make the required preparations to receive or create it, as if it were impossible to fail.

You build your port and wait for your ships to come in. You set your stage and wait for the actors and audience to arrive. You dig your trenches and wait for the rain to fall. The famous line in the movie, *Field of Dreams*, says it all: "Build it, and they will come."

Here are two accounts that illustrate this type of receptive preparation.

The first is an example of ordering a kitchen fridge. Once it's been ordered, you need to prepare an area in the kitchen with appropriate electrical accessibility where the fridge will be placed. The fridge cannot reside in your house or apartment until an area has been prepared especially and specifically for it.

The simple, take-home message of this example is to prepare for your success as though it is a *fait accompli*, acting as if you knew you can't fail. You've ordered it. It's on its way. All you need to do is prepare for it to arrive.

The second example of receptive preparation is of anticipated love. A story I once heard was of a single woman who desired a husband and a family. She lived alone at the time but actively prepared for the arrival of her as yet unknown future husband by purchasing a double-bed, extra clothes hangers, bathroom towels, and even an extra toothbrush, which she kept in a rinsing glass next to her bathroom sink.

She also took it another step further. She realised that she had to not only prepare her physical surroundings for his arrival, but also her mental attitude. When she looked in the mirror, she trained herself to see a married wife, not a spinster. She knew she had to 'be married' in her imagination and act like a wife, including all the positive emotions she anticipated having, to prepare for her upcoming wedding, which she had no doubt would happen. Even though she had not yet met her future husband, she actively prepared herself by thinking, feeling and acting as if he were already living with her.

Neville Goddard described this type of receptive preparation as coming *from* the position of the wish fulfilled (having/receiving), not the position of wishing *for* the fulfillment of the wish (wanting/needing). Your heart must be embedded in the imagined outcome. You must feel the future in this instant, this present moment of Now. In other words, you come *from* the end you have in mind, which includes thinking, feeling, and behaving as having already achieved your goal. You act in the real world what you imagine you have already achieved. That is, you need to *be* in your mind before you *do* in the physical world.

Imagination and intentions come first. Then feelings and emotions. Then actions and behaviours.

> *You create a bridge to your future intentions by bringing them into the present moment through your thoughts, feelings, and actions.*

The examples of ordering a refrigerator and the woman preparing for her future husband illustrate the need for a degree of faith and belief when employing receptive preparation. Or more to the point, a degree of *active* faith. You anticipate your success by actively preparing and arranging your life, your lifestyle, and your house in advance *as if your success was already manifest,* as if it were already a *fait accompli.*

If you don't, you're actually preparing to be let down. You have *inactive* faith. You're preparing for failure.

One of my life-coaching clients, Michael G., had saved quite a large sum of money that he was putting aside for any opportunity that might arise to leave his day job and venture forth on his entrepreneurial dream. We were working to identify his long-term goal of establishing a wellbeing studio for yoga, Pilates, personal fitness, and personal-development workshops. An opportunity to rent a studio for a good price had come up in a desirable location, but he was hesitating at signing the rental agreement.

THE POWER OF COMMITMENT

"I'm not sure it's the right thing to do," he said. "What if I need the money for something else?"

"So, are you preparing for things that can go wrong?" I asked. "Or are you preparing for things that can go right?"

He sat back and nodded with understanding. It was true, he admitted, he had been saving money for 'a rainy day' just in case he needed it if things turned for the worse.

Of course, saving for a rainy day isn't wrong. But if that becomes your excuse for not reaching for your dream, then fear has taken hold of your mind and you will most likely procrastinate and not grab the opportunities that present to you. If fear predominates your thinking, procrastination will dominate your behaviours, and your life will be a reflection of your lack of action.

Henry Wadsworth Longfellow, one of the most well-known and admired poets of 19th Century America, whose works include *The Song of Hiawatha* and the epic poem *Evangeline*, put it this way:

A man's life is a history to his fears.

Fear causes inactive faith. It prevents you from taking action on your hopes, dreams, and desires. Inaction over a lifetime curtails not only your potential but also your success, and when you look back at your life you see a story of what could have been—a history of unfulfilled desires and underused talent that has been written with the pen of fear.

But the future is not yet written, it's a blank page, so there is an antidote to fear. There is a way through it, and that's arming yourself with active faith.

The pen is mightier than the sword, as they say, and there's always time to rewrite your history the way you want it to turn out. So why not look ahead, plan what you want to do, and write the remaining pages of your life with the pen of active faith?

A simple, everyday example of active faith that you can implement almost immediately is preparing for your next holiday. This brings us back to my road trip from Denver to Las Vegas. I had actively prepared for my arrival at my hotel on The Strip by bringing my backpack and wallet. It's what we all do when we go on holiday. We pack our bags with clothes, swimming bathers, toiletries, and maybe a passport and other items we will need when we get to our destination—we *prepare in advance* for our successful arrival.

We know exactly where we're going—we can even see the hotel or apartment in our minds, inhale the aromas and hear the noises we expect to encounter when we get there—and we just get on with it and do it. This is the 'future pacing' that we've discussed previously, and which we'll discuss further in just a moment when we talk about *Consolidating Your Opportunity*. For now, we generally do this future pacing on autopilot, without paying it too much thought. We expect to arrive safely at our hotel or lodgings with a high degree of certainty, and we envisage ourselves doing the things we want to do on holiday with just as much expectancy. We prepare for our holiday success as a matter of fact, as though it is already written in our holiday diary.

We imagine what we want and we do it, although more often than not it's an unconscious and unthinking process, almost humdrum. But think of all the times you've succeeded this way, more unconsciously than consciously, and imagine how much more you could achieve and how much more success you could enjoy if you just put a little bit more conscious thought into your intentions and desires.

How wonderful, then, would it be if success in life was as matter of fact as driving or flying or bussing to your holiday destination? How wonderful would it be to expect to arrive at where you want to go in life as easy as arriving at your hotel?

It's not as far-fetched as you think. You can achieve the success you want if you're more conscious about it, but there is a little bit more work to do before success comes as easy as booking a holiday. You have to make it a daily habit to dig into that goldmind of yours and actively think about what you need to do. Success doesn't come without thought. It doesn't come without brainpower. It doesn't come without foresight and imagination and planning.

It doesn't also tend to come without preparation either. It doesn't come without constructively developing the skills or gaining the education required to sidestep the barriers of entry of your desired career, or without the faith and belief that you'll receive the rewards you're working for.

Which leads to the final point, that your success won't come without taking action, without putting in effort, without persevering.

THE POWER OF PERSEVERANCE

There is no such thing as effortless success. Very few, if any, have achieved success on their first attempt.

The master, as we have discussed before, has failed more times than the beginner has tried. Masters know that success waits for you to take the first step. They also know there's no easy way, that the reason faith without works is dead is because you have to take some form of action to bridge the gap between where you are now and the destination you want to reach. You have to put in the effort. You have to persevere.

This means that sometimes you have to make a choice between feeling comfortable and making progress. It means you have to get comfortable with feeling uncomfortable. Yes, progress is hard. Yes, life is difficult. Yes, living your dream means making sacrifices. But it's invariably the one who perseveres who gets to taste the champagne at the end of the race.

Consider this. If you turn on a tap for a few minutes you might release enough water to fill half a bath. But if you let that tap drip every ten seconds over a month, that's a massive 70 litres (or about 18 gallons). That's the power of perseverance. Slow and steady. Drip... drip... drip... drip...

Consistency, therefore, is key. Consistency drives progress. Inconsistency leads to regress. But you can't have consistency without perseverance. So giving up is not an option. There will be obstacles in your way along your journey to success, but set your course and keep going no matter what. Be as Winston Churchill said, never give in, never, never, never, never.

That's what successful people do: they set their course and simply don't give in. It means they fail more often, but it also means they succeed more too. Michael Jordan claimed he missed 10,000 shots in his basketball career, and that's why he was a success. Colonel Sanders' recipe for Kentucky Fried Chicken was rejected 1009 times before he found a willing backer.

They were resilient. They persevered. They used failures as stepping-stones to their success.

PLANNING, PREPARATION & PERSEVERANCE

In your intention to become the person you want to be and do the things you really want to do, planning, preparation, and perseverance will be required. As such, there are three main conditions that you will need to be mindful of and seek to develop:

1. Your *destination and aims* in life.
2. Your *attitude toward opportunity*.
3. Your *desire and dedication* toward your goals.

Developing and maintaining your skills in these areas is essential if your intent is to be more successful and impactful. Which is why

THE POWER OF COMMITMENT

developing your skills of Planning, Preparation & Perseverance is the fourth Power Habit of Success. In Part II, III and IV, you began developing the first three Power Habits of Self-Assuredness & Self-Belief, Courage & Confidence, and Other People Thinking, using this formula:

- -> Awakening your Imagination, Intention, and Attitude superpowers.
- -> Getting clarity on your identity of who you are and want to be—I Am.
- -> Igniting your motivation—I Will.
- -> Tapping into your conviction—I Can.

These three fundamental components—I Am, I Will, I Can—have been used to build the Power Elements of Faith, Valour, and Value. These same three components will now be used to build the Power Element of Commitment, which you will need to utilise throughout your journey of success.

Business coaches tell us the Number One reason 50-80% of small businesses fail in the first five years of operation is not cashflow, not production issues, not staffing, but *commitment*. Of course there are multiple headwinds a business owner must face when starting out, but it is the failure of small business owners to commit 100% to their business that is the main reason their business doesn't succeed.

Nothing less than 100% commitment will do the job. Not 50% commitment, not 75% commitment, not even 98% commitment. Only 100% commitment to the business will make the difference between being in those 50-80% of businesses that fail or being in the 20-50% of businesses that will still be around in 5 years' time and thriving.

The same is true for the dreams you have for the future and the goals you set. Your success depends on how committed you are, and only 100% commitment will do the job. Not 50% commitment, not 75% commitment, not even 98% commitment. Only 100% commitment to your dreams and goals will make the difference between failing and disappointment, or the successful accomplishment and enjoying the fruits of your work.

The parable of *The Chicken and the Pig* illustrates the difference between being fully committed to the success of something and having an interest or investment in it:

> Two friends, a pig and a chicken, wanted to go into partnership with each other and start a business. They discussed many options and settled on starting a cafe, where they would focus on breakfast meals.
>
> The pig agreed that he would provide the bacon, and the chicken agreed that she would provide the eggs.
>
> Both were important to the production of the breakfast meals, but the business failed because only the pig was 100% committed to its success, whereas the chicken only had a vested interest.

For the pig, there was no other option but for the venture to succeed. For the chicken, however, the success of the venture was neither here nor there.

So, how much of yourself are you putting into the fulfillment of your dreams? How much of yourself are you committing to your success?

Are you like the pig, fully committed, or are you more like the chicken, with just a vested interest?

THE POWER OF COMMITMENT

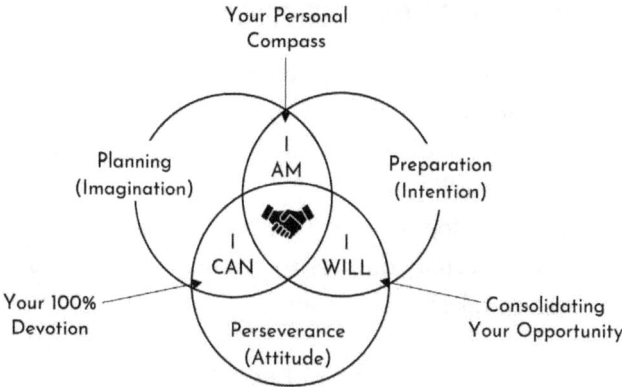

FIGURE 22: Power Element–Commitment

The above diagram explains how your Imagination, Intention, and Attitude align to solidify your commitment:

- -> Identity: the overlap where your Imagination and Intention align is where you orientate yourself and set *your personal compass*—your 'I Am'.
- -> Purpose: the overlap where your Intention and Attitude align is where you *consolidate your attitude* toward opportunity—your 'I Will'.
- -> Conviction: the overlap where your Attitude and Imagination align is where you *devote 100%* to your dreams—your 'I Can'.

The commitment to who you want to be and what you want to do is in the central overlap where the three components of your Personal Compass (I Am), Attitude to Opportunity (I Will), and Devotion to Your Dreams (I Can) merge and align as one Power Element called Commitment.

The Power Habit of Planning, Preparation & Perseverance is how you develop this Power Element. It's how you commit to making your life a success.

IDENTITY: SETTING YOUR PERSONAL COMPASS—I AM

Your destination and aims in life are like a personal compass you need to set for yourself. In a sense, they are like your True North—they determine the direction you will follow throughout much of the course of your life.

Without setting your direction, which way will you go? Without an internal compass to guide you, how will you know which path to take?

FIGURE 23:   Your Personal Compass–I Am

You won't know, so you'll end up drifting through life and risk missing out on opportunities because you haven't planned or prepared for them. Worse, like Derek the Dragonfly, you risk being omitted from the pages of your own history because you failed to make yourself 'necessary to the story'.

Setting your personal compass means knowing exactly what you want. It means knowing what boxes in life you want to tick before you see your last sunset. You plan and you prepare. You use your Imagination to plan who you want to be and plan what you want to do. You use your Intention to prepare yourself for the journey.

THE POWER OF COMMITMENT

So the first step of committing yourself to your journey is to set your personal compass and orientate yourself with your True North. But along the way to your intended destination, there are milestones you need to reach, goals you need to accomplish, targets you need to hit. These are the visible markers of your invisible destination.

Just like the 750-mile drive from Denver to Las Vegas. The highway my friend and I were cruising was marked with signposts indicating how far my friend and I had left to go—600 miles, 550 miles, 500 miles—until we finally reached the outskirts of the desert city. They were visible markers of a destination that was a long way over the horizon and out of sight, giving us confidence that we were heading in the right direction and keeping on track.

Knowing how far we still had to drive meant we could also pace ourselves and take appropriate rest breaks. We could even estimate the time we'd arrive at our destination, assuming we maintained consistent speed and weren't delayed by any roadworks or breakdowns, or had to detour for any unforeseen reason.

Additionally, not only did each signpost indicate how far we had left to drive, but also, through inference, how far we had come. They were, literally, milestones along our journey. They were goals we needed to reach, targets we need to hit, to reach our destination.

Unfortunately, the mistake we all make is to try to leap forward to our destination and skip all the annoying milestones. We just want to get there. Quickly. Now!

But that's not how success works. You can't just beam over and teleport to your destination like Captain Kirk on the USS Starship *Enterprise*. You can only arrive at your destination one milestone at a time, one goal at a time, in order and in sequence. Remember, success is a progressive realisation of a worthy ideal. The word 'progressive' means you have to move forward, you have to make progress. You have to pass each milestone, reach each goal, hit every target.

Your True North

In a way, the realisation of your worthy goal is systematic. It's procedural. But before you set off on your journey, you first need to orientate yourself with your destination, your True North. I've just mentioned Captain Kirk, so let's use him as an example of how to use your personal compass to orientate yourself. We'll do this by having an imaginary interview with the legendary character. Here we go:

> Q: Captain Kirk, who are you?
>
> Kirk: *I am a hero.*
>
> Q: What do you do?
>
> Kirk: *I save humans (and aliens) from disaster.*
>
> Q: Why do you do it?
>
> Kirk: *To make the universe a safer place.*
>
> Q: How do you do it?
>
> Kirk: *I boldly go where no-one has gone before.*

Despite the fictional nature of this interview, let's analyse these answers and see how Captain Kirk can help you set your personal compass and achieve out-of-this-world success.

To the question of 'Who are you?', Kirk's answer is not, "I'm the captain of the starship *Enterprise*." Which would have been technically correct, but that's not how he feels about himself. When he looks in the mirror, he sees a hero. He feels he is a hero. There's passion and emotion and enthusiasm to being Captain Kirk, the hero.

Do you have that same passion and enthusiasm to being you? Recall the exercise in finding your 1-word in Chapter 5. Kirk's 1-word is 'hero'. He aligns with that 1-word and identifies with it as the core of who he is. He is committed to it. He does not tie his identity to what he does or to his achievements, he ties his identity to who and what he wants to be, heroic.

The next question in our imaginary interview with Kirk asks him to determine what he actually does. For Kirk, besides all the other duties captains of spaceships have to do, he sees his main role and duty as saving humans and aliens from disaster. Which fits perfectly with his vision of himself as a galactic hero. It's what he does.

How he reacts and responds to what is happening around him is directly related to how he sees himself. His behaviour is heroic because that's who he sees in the mirror. Likewise, how you react or respond to what's going on around you is an expression of how you see yourself in this moment. Your reactions and responses therefore define who you say you are. Every waking moment, then, every situation, is an opportunity to tell the world who you are and who you want to be. What you do is an expression of who you are.

The third question relates to purpose and motivation: Why does Kirk do what he does?

To make the universe a safer place, that's why. It's his reason for living. It's what gets him out of his captain's quarters and onto the bridge of the *Enterprise* every day. It's his purpose for being. His *raison d'etre*.

This is his Why? and it helps shape the image he has of himself. It energises and motivates him to do what he wants to do.

This is also the reason your 'Why?' is so vital, because it helps clarify the first two steps in setting your personal compass:

1. Defining who you are (your image and vision of what you want to grow into), and
2. Determining exactly what it is you want to do and achieve.

Your 'Who, What, Why' reinforce and support each other like three sides of a triangle: without one, the triangle collapses.

The final question in our imaginary interview establishes how you want to go about your day-to-day life. For Captain Kirk, it's to boldly go where no-one has gone before. He strides forward into the unknown, breaching the horizon at warp speed.

Because that's how heroes do what they need to do.

Your Personal Compass

The aim of setting your personal compass is to clarify your Who, What, Why, and How? This way, you can aim for your True North and maximise your chances of living the life you want, the way you want, how you want, which is success in anyone's language.

Let's have a look at how some historical figures might have answered these same questions.

<u>Nelson Mandela</u>

Q: Nelson Mandela, who are you?

Mandela: *I am a liberator.*

Q: What do you do?

Mandela: *I liberate my people from oppression.*

Q: Why do you do it?

Mandela: *To unite my country.*

Q: How do you do it?

Mandela: *I take the long walk to freedom.*

Buddha

Q: Buddha, who are you?

Buddha: *I am awake.*

Q: What do you do?

Buddha: *I help humanity escape the illusion of separation.*

Q: Why do you do it?

Buddha: *To end suffering.*

Q: How do you do it?

Buddha: *Through compassion and loving kindness.*

Abraham Lincoln

Q: Abraham Lincoln, who are you?

Lincoln: *I am an emancipator.*

Q: What do you do?

Lincoln: *I free the slaves in my country.*

Q: Why do you do it?

Lincoln: *To create a free, just, and united society.*

Q: How do you do it?

Lincoln: *With malice toward none, with charity for all, with firmness in the right as God gives us to see the right.*

Here's how I personally answer these very same questions:

Q: Scott Zarcinas, who are you?

A: *I am a transformational writer and coach.*

Q: What do you do?

A: *I help people awaken to the truth of themselves.*

Q: Why do you do it?
A: *So everyone can truly know life and have it abundantly.*
Q: How do you do it?
A: *By connecting people with the answers that they are looking for.*

Now, how would you answer those questions and set your personal compass?

Q: Who are you?
A: _____

Q: What do you do?
A: _____

Q: Why do you do it?
A: _____

Q: How do you do it?
A: _____

12 DARING TO DREAM

PURPOSE: CONSOLIDATING YOUR OPPORTUNITY—I WILL

THE NEXT COMPONENT of developing the Power Habit of Planning, Preparation & Perseverance and building the Power Element of Commitment is to consolidate your opportunity.

There is opportunity in every day. But to see opportunities you first must develop the right mindset to be open to them, you must acknowledge that opportunities arise for everybody and not only for a select few. Then you must seek them out. You must be vigilant for opportunity and ready yourself to grab them with both hands. Only then can you consolidate your opportunities.

How you develop the mindset of consolidating your opportunities is by aligning your Intention with your Attitude. This means to align your intention to seek out opportunity—vigilance—with the attitude of openness, of not having a closed or judgemental attitude to what presents itself to you. The extent to which you consolidate your opportunities is best achieved through your willingness to seize the opportunity in every day—what the Romans called *Carpe Opportunitas*.

> *Your attitude toward opportunity determines the amplitude of your opportunity.*

If you believe only rich people have opportunity, you will not see the opportunities all around you because your attitude blinds you to them. If you believe only men have opportunity, you will not hear the opportunities all around you because your attitude deafens you to them. If you believe only white people have opportunity, you will not sense the opportunities all around you because your attitude desensitises you to them.

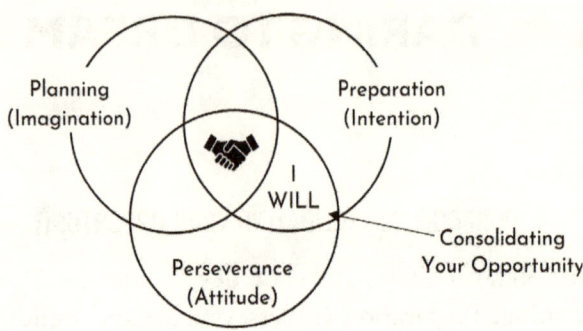

FIGURE 24:   Consolidating Your Opportunity–I Will

In regard to making the most of your opportunities in life, as much as anything else, your attitude toward opportunity is *the* defining factor in exploiting all the wonderful opportunities that exist for you.

A closed attitude toward opportunity leads to missed opportunities. An open attitude toward opportunity leads to kissed opportunities.

It doesn't matter if the world is in recession or depression, or if the world is in riding high in boom times, opportunities always abound and it's your attitude that determines whether or not you cash in on them.

Carpe Opportunitas

There was a time in my youth when I had a pretty closed attitude toward opportunity. I thought opportunity happened only to others, especially the rich and privileged, not to me.

As a white male graduating from a private school and going on to study medicine at university, I was stone-cold oblivious to the irony of my attitude. Entitled, some would say, but I didn't feel entitled. I was the 'poor kid in a rich school' and, as such,

I felt poor despite my surroundings and privilege. I saw friends and colleagues travelling overseas and skiing during the holidays. While they were having fun, I stayed at home in my working-class suburb on the edge of town or worked in my grandfather's roadhouse to save a bit of money that other school kids didn't need to do. Not that I wasn't grateful for my schooling, I most certainly was, and still am, but the comparisons between the wealth of other kids' families and the struggles of my own, where money was always tight, were magnified in a private school environment.

So, despite my privileged education, I kind of felt poor and underprivileged, which reflected my lack of insight and teenage entitlement. I felt opportunity was only for the rich kids, and that excluded me. I was resigned to my lot and the way of the world. Essentially, I had victimised myself, and I carried this 'woe is me' attitude into my university days.

It wasn't until the final two years of university as a 5th- and 6th-year medical student that my attitude began to slowly (and painfully) change from 'passive victim' to 'active victor'. Up until then, I rarely took the first step to get what I wanted. I invariably waited for other people to give me what I wanted and was thus invariably disappointed when they didn't come up with the goods. I hadn't yet learned that if you don't ask, you don't get.

Looking back, I had an embedded attitude of powerlessness and helplessness. Other people, rich people, people in authority, held the power and not me. They could do whatever they wanted. They had all the money. They had all the opportunities. They had all the fun.

Not me. I was powerless. I had to make do with whatever came my way and scrap for any limited opportunity that might happen to fall at my feet, if someone else didn't grab it first. Then an incident happened that caused me to reassess my attitude to 'the way of the world' and my victimised attitude toward myself.

The final years of medical training require a lot of on-site attendance on the wards and in the emergency department from 9 to 5 Monday to Friday, and even some weekend and overnight assignments. The hours are long and tiring, which is why most hospitals have a student mess tucked away in the building, a place where exhausted students can slump in a chair and put their feet up for a while. A place to catch up with what's happening with friends and colleagues, have a bite to eat, and even catch the news or a soap opera on TV before heading back to the wards.

The old Royal Adelaide Hospital where I trained in the late 80s and early 90s had a student mess on the 7th floor of the main building. The room was spacious and overlooked the front entrance, but it was tired and in dire need of a coat of paint. The chairs puffed dust whenever you plonked down on them, and the faded lounge cushions had a permanent indentation from years of use. Despite its dreariness, there was always a constant stream of students coming in and out, a little oasis where you could put the mayhem of the medical and surgical wards out of sight and out of earshot for just a while to catch your breath and settle your mind. But it lacked the most important thing of all—a pinball machine.

For the good part of nine months, I pleaded with no avail to get the student committee to approve the installation of a pinball machine in the mess room. The committee members were in charge of everything that was allowed and not allowed in the mess. They had the power and I, because I wasn't on the committee, didn't. I tried to reason with them and convince them of the benefits of having a pinball machine would have on student morale, but they just weren't interested. Everything I said fell on deaf ears. I was frustrated, and as the months went on I became angrier and resentful, as much at their reluctance to act on my requests as I was with my powerless to do something about it.

Then one lunchtime, while I was mulling over the utter

unreasonableness of the student committee and the unfairness of life in general, a voice in my head said, "Scott, why don't you just do it yourself?"

Why not? I nodded to myself. *Why don't I just go and buy a pinball machine and put it in the mess myself?*

Spurred with sudden enthusiasm, I quickly tracked down my good friend and fellow medical student, Mark F., who thought it was a fantastic idea. We rushed out of the hospital and drove to the nearest pinball repairer and purchased a second-hand pinball machine. *Mata Hari* was beautiful, and she only cost A$200. That evening, when most students had left the hospital, we transported the pinball machine to the Royal Adelaide Hospital, took it up the elevator, and installed it into the empty corner of the student mess.

It was an instant success. Students, mostly males of course, crowded around the machine for hours on end. Even better, the student committee didn't say a word. The machine took 20c pieces and by the end of the week we had over A$100 in silver coins, which we lugged down the lobby escalator to the onsite bank and deposited into our newly-opened, joint savings account. By the end of the second week, the machine had paid itself off, and within a month we had bought our second machine. Two months after that, we bought a third machine, and for the next two years my friend and I pocketed more than A$100 per week each in profit, which more than paid for our social life and kept us very happy.

To put this in perspective, I would have needed A$100,000 in a savings account working at 5% interest to receive the equivalent amount each year. Or in a lower-interest environment, I'd need A$500,000 working at 1% per annum. Remember, this all happened during the recession of the early 90s, when jobs were scarce and businesses were shutting down and boarding up.

I tell this story to highlight two points. First, I was blind to the opportunity of making a passive income through pinball machines for nine months because of my 'poor me' victim mentality. Because of my attitude that it was someone else's responsibility to provide what I wanted, I missed seeing the opportunity that was waiting for me like an eager puppy in that empty corner of the mess room. This first lesson follows Seneca's advice that luck happens when preparation meets opportunity. This, then, is the lesson I learned and have been mindful of for over 30 years:

> *When I was prepared to take responsibility for myself and what I wanted, the opportunity unveiled itself.*

My ventures into entrepreneurship also revealed something extraordinary: *opportunity is everywhere.*

That is the second point. There's always opportunity. No matter your economic or social environment, no matter your job or what upbringing you have. Opportunity is as omnipresent as the air we breathe. Not a day goes by without opportunity being within your grasp. All you need to do is to make sure you prepare yourself with an open attitude. Then you're ready to seize your opportunity and turn it into success.

The Rule of 5

One way to prepare for your opportunities is to follow The Rule of 5. The Rule of 5 simply states that you do five things every day that will prepare you for future opportunities. Everyone will have their own take on this rule. Everyone will have their own list of five things to do based on who they want to become and what they want to achieve.

Here are my Rule of 5 things that I do everyday to prepare for the opportunities that will present themselves to me:

My Rule of 5: THINK

   T: Type and Write
   H: How? Questions
   I: Use my Imagination Superpower
   N: Network and Build Relationships
   K: Keep an Ideas Bank

<u>T: Type and Write</u>
Because I'm a writer at heart, I need to do what writers do, which is write. I sit down at the keyboard and type something every day. Some days it's barely a few hundred words. Other days it's upwards of 5,000 words. The number of words on any given day isn't as important as the intention of typing and writing every single day. I've got to do as Babe Ruth would, I've got to keep swinging. I've got to keep standing up at the plate knowing the Law of Averages will work in my favour. I'll hit more home runs that way.

<u>H: How? Questions</u>
How questions are better than why questions. Why questions tend to come from a mindset of victimisation. Why me? Why does this always happen? Why can't I do anything right? Why am I always the one missing out?

Why me? sounds like whining. Whining doesn't get you anywhere. So it's better to turn your 'whys' into 'hows'. How me? How can I make it happen? How can I do better? How can I make sure I don't miss out?

How questions will bring you from victim to victor much quicker than why questions.

I: Use my Imagination Superpower

One of the great joys of writing is that, by default, you must use your imagination. You use your imagination to plan what you want to write. You use your imagination to tell stories. You use your imagination to paint word pictures for your readers.

But there are many uses for imagination. Anything creative, like playing music, singing, painting, sculpting, acting, employs imagination. So too does everyday chores like gardening, grocery shopping, dishwashing, making the beds, ironing the clothes. These things seem so mundane, however, that you probably feel as though they don't take much imagination. Yet they do. Especially when you are present in the moment and vigilant to the process of using your imagination, and when you keep asking yourself how you can improve the way you do these mundane tasks.

Your Imagination superpower is a great asset for anything you do. Strengthen it every day with the little things you do and it will be fit and strong for the big things you want to do.

N: Network

Everything you do is built on relationships you have with other people. Every aspect of your 7 Life Segments is built on relationships. You family, friends, work. Your health and wellbeing. Your money and finances. Your learning and education. Your fun and adventure. Even your spirituality and ethics. Everything involves having a relationship with somebody else, even if it's just a simple transaction of buying groceries or a bus ticket.

Business coaches tell us that success in business is first achieved through growing your network. Your business is built on your network. Businesses that do well and grow and are solid even through recession times have a solid network. They build and maintain their relationships with their customers, staff, and other collaborating businesses. They build loyalty and actively nurture their customer base.

Likewise, your personal and professional success will benefit greatly from your network. You will benefit greatly when you build and nurture your relationships.

Simple things like phoning a friend, texting a family member who lives interstate or overseas, emailing updates to your business community, organising a coffee catchup or evening drinks with people you haven't seen for a while.

There are many things you can do every day to grow and sustain your network. The key is to be consistent.

K: Keep an Ideas Bank

The wonderful thing about ideas is that they happen all the time. The unfortunate thing about ideas is that they happen all the time.

They happen while you're eating breakfast. They happen while you are in the shower. They happen while you're commuting to work. They happen while you are asleep.

Which is why it's important to keep a diary or notepad handy, or any recording device for that matter. Many of my ideas pop up during morning meditation, and I know that if I don't write the ideas down straight away I'll forget them before I finish my session. Some ideas for books I've even dreamed, so waking up at 3am or 4am and writing brief notes in a notepad I keep next to my bed has been hugely beneficial to remembering the dream when I wake up the next morning.

I also get great ideas from listening to other people. Even during brief conversations with friends, family, or clients, they will often say something, or I'll reply with something, that I know will be valuable in a book. So I write it down.

I also read articles on the internet, or even social media. They will often reference a research article, or a famous quote, or a book I haven't read, so I'll be sure to write down the reference to use later.

I'm also disciplined in typing all my ideas into a Word

document and storing them in an ideas folder on my computer. Misplacing a notepad with all your great ideas that you've recorded is something you'd do well to avoid, a frustration I've personally experienced.

The examples I've given are mainly related to my writing. But the concept of keeping an ideas bank can be used for anything you set yourself to achieve. If you're thinking of renovating the kitchen, you can keep an ideas bank of great pictures and concepts you happen to see. If you're thinking of travelling, you can keep an ideas bank of places you want to see, places other people tell you about that you haven't heard of before and sound great. If you're in business, you can keep an ideas bank of great marketing strategies that you see and hear.

So keeping an ideas bank is a great habit to prepare for future opportunities.

TAKING YOUR OPPORTUNITIES

Billionaire entrepreneur, Richard Branson, is cited as saying opportunities are like buses: there's always another one coming along. You just have to be on the lookout for them. If you're not looking for buses (opportunities), you won't see them, no matter how big and bright they are.

But know this, which is probably the third lesson: *opportunity doesn't discriminate*. It doesn't ignore anybody based on their gender, sexual orientation, religious beliefs, colour of their skin, age, or abilities.

If you believe it does, how did Oprah, a black woman, become one of the most successful human beings on the planet?

She didn't have it easy. She suffered racism and sexism, and even tragedy on more than one occasion. But she prepared herself and she took the opportunity when she saw it. She made her own luck. She created her own success.

No, opportunity doesn't discriminate, but what it does do is present itself in many guises. This means that opportunity presents itself differently to different people. What is an opportunity for me is not an opportunity for you, and vice versa. What presents as an opportunity for you doesn't present itself as an opportunity for me.

Opportunity is a personalised gift from Life, the gift that never stops giving.

Your opportunities are only meant for you. In fact, I don't even see your opportunities. They are invisible to me. Your opportunities are only visible to you.

But you will only see your opportunities when you look for them through the right lens. The right lens, of course, is the right mindset. If you don't have the right mindset, you won't see your opportunities. You won't even recognise them as opportunities. The great inventor, Thomas Edison, pointed out that opportunity is usually dressed in overalls and looks like hard work, which is why most people miss it or don't recognise it.

The right mindset to see your opportunities as they present to you is to have the widest lens possible. Not shuttered. Not tinted. Not closed. Not blind. But open, and you can gauge how open your mindset is when you have these three attitudes, and believe that:

1. Your Opportunities are Unlimited in Number and in *Guise*.
2. Your Opportunities are Your Personal *Gift* from Life.
3. Your Opportunities *Grow* with Your Expectations.

Just as your mobile phones are connected to a cellular network, I call these attitudes the 3G Network—Guise, Gift, Growth—because *your attitude is how you communicate with your opportunity.*

3G #1: Your Opportunities are Unlimited in Number and in Guise

Do you believe your opportunities are unlimited? Do you believe your opportunities are all around you? Do you believe your opportunities come in many sizes, shapes, and forms?

Successful people do. They see a wonderful world full of unlimited opportunities. They see them everywhere, in every size, shape, and form. They know that for every problem there's a solution, and in that solution is their opportunity to grow, to profit, to learn, to become better than before that problem existed.

How, then, can we see what they see? We have the same five senses of sight, hearing, touch, taste, and smell, so what's preventing us from seeing the opportunity in every problem?

Judgement.

Your judgement of 'what is' is what stops you from seeing 'what really is'. Your judgement of 'what is' blinds you to the truth of 'what is'. It is the plank in your eye, which is like a drawn curtain—you can't see what's outside.

The Sufis call this your 'permanent hidden prejudice', which is the filter through which you view yourself, your world, and everything else that happens in and around you. Your permanent hidden prejudice is how you think the world should be, not what is presented to you. It is often the underlying cause of all your frustrations, resistance, anger, jealousy, and fears. It is often the very reason you struggle to live the life you want, the way you want, how you want.

The parable of the *Nun in the Desert* illustrates this point.

> A nun was driving alone to her mission settlement through the Australian outback when she heard a loud bang and then noticed steam pouring through the hood of the car. She pulled over to the side of the dirt road just as the engine seized and died.

She knew traffic along the road was very infrequent, but being a woman of faith, she was not afraid. "God will provide," she said.

As the hot midday sun beat down on her, a motorbike rider stopped and asked if she needed a ride.

"Thank you, but no, God will provide," she said.

The night came and the hot sun rose again the next morning. By the afternoon, nobody else had driven by and she had finished her last bottle of water, but she was a woman of faith and she was not afraid.

That evening, a cloud of dust appeared on the horizon and soon a car pulled up next to her. "Do you need a lift?" asked the driver.

"Thank you, but no, God will provide," she said.

On the third day, thirsty and hungry and barely able to stand, a farmer's truck came to a halt in a cloud of dirt and dust. "Do you need a lift?" asked the farmer.

"Thank you, but no, God will provide," she said, her throat dry and husky.

The next day, under the scorching sun, the nun perished and went to heaven. Annoyed that God had not provided for her in her hour of need, she demanded an immediate counsel with Him.

"Why did you not help me?" she asked.

"Goodness me," said God, "I sent you a motorbike, a car, and a truck. What else did you expect?"

When we have preconceived ideas of what opportunities should look like, we often fail to see them when they come to us.

Preconception often causes missed perception.
Just as the motorbike, the car, and the farmer's truck were invisible opportunities to the nun, you risk missing out on the big opportunities Life sends your way if you demand that they take a certain size, shape, or form.

3G #2: Your Opportunities are Your Personal Gift from Life

In Ben Stiller's remake of the movie, *The Secret Life of Walter Mitty* (2013), there is a pivotal scene where he, Walter Mitty, is faced with a defining choice that will impact his life forever. He must decide on taking a risky, but ultimately rewarding, opportunity to find what he's been searching for, or give up and go back to his old job in New York as a negative asset manager at *Life* magazine. He is at a crossroad. One way leads to an uncertain but potentially liberating future. The other returns him to his old ways, a lost, confused daydreamer.

The irony is, Walter Mitty works for *Life* but he isn't living. He is approaching middle age and his job is under threat when an outside team is hired to restructure the workforce in line with moving the publication from the traditional print model to an online digital model. The magazine still uses negatives to process their photos and images, and Walter is tasked with producing the final cover image for the last ever print run for the magazine. The only problem is, he's lost the negative.

This sparks the frantic search for the magazine's lead photographer, Sean O'Connell, played by Sean Penn, who could be anywhere in the world at any particular time. The contrast between the two characters is stark. Sean O'Connell is an adventure-seeking, risk-taking, life-loving nature photographer who sometimes won't even press the shutter button to capture a rare photograph if he's absorbed in the moment of being alive. Walter Mitty is a safety-seeking, risk-averse, scared-of-life, middle-employee who works in the dark basement of his building and won't even ask the woman he is in love with, Cheryl Melhoff (played by Kristen Wiig), out on a date. Sean O'Connell lives life to the full; Walter Mitty daydreams of it.

But circumstances push Walter Mitty to locate Sean O'Connell, wherever in the world he is. The deadline for the final print run of the magazine is looming, and his boss is demanding the cover image. Sean O'Connell doesn't have a mobile phone and is constantly on the move, so he can't be contacted by conventional means. Walter Mitty reluctantly follows a set of clues to Greenland, where he believes Sean O'Connell has boarded a fishing boat. It's at this point that Walter Mitty comes face to face with his own fears of living.

He meets a helicopter pilot in a bar in a small fishing village who tells him the boat he is looking for is just offshore. The bad news is that the ship's radio communication is broken and so Walter Mitty can't speak to Sean O'Connell via radio or satellite phone. The good news for Walter Mitty is that the helicopter pilot is delivering the radio parts to the boat that day. Walter can get a ride with him if he wants and speak directly to Sean O'Connell.

Unfortunately, the helicopter pilot is so drunk he can barely stand without teetering over. But he's still going to fly the helicopter to the fishing boat and deliver the parts, and Walter Mitty is still welcome to come with him.

Scared for his life, Walter declines to get on board the helicopter. Walter Mitty watches through the window as the pilot gets into the cockpit and settles behind the controls. He is torn between jumping into the passenger seat or staying behind, resigned to watching the only chance he has of retrieving the negative and his reputation disappear over the horizon with the drunk helicopter pilot.

So Walter Mitty does what he has always done when life corners him and forces him to make a choice: he daydreams.

In his vivid imagination, he sees Cheryl Melhoff enter the bar with a guitar and start singing David Bowie's *'Space Oddity'*. She strums the guitar and begins the song: *"Ground control to Major Tom... Ground control to Major Tom... Take your protein pills and put your helmet on..."*

This becomes the most pivotal moment in Walter Mitty's life. Does he stay or does he go? Does he continue fearing life or does he break from his past and risk it all on this one moment?

When Cheryl gets to the end of the first verse and sings, *"Commencing countdown, engines on... Check ignition and may God's love be with you..."* something inside him gives. Like an elastic cord that has been stretched so far it no longer has any more resistance, Mitty snaps. He is finally freed from all the constraints of his past and free to run towards his destiny.

Walter Mitty has finally broken through his fears of living and he dashes toward the helicopter to embrace his new future. He is a new man. He is changed, and not only has his whole future changed from this moment forward, but his whole world has now changed.

This movie, and especially this scene, is a great illustration of the message we have been repeating throughout this book:

> *When your inner world changes, your outer world changes.*

Katherine Mansfield was a modernist writer and poet who grew up in New Zealand and lived in England in the late 19th and early 20th Centuries. She is considered by some literary critics as one of the best short story writers of all time, a woman who pioneered the short story genre in the early 20th Century. She once made a poignant comment on how our attitudes affect our world:

> *Could we change our attitude, we should not only see life differently, but life itself would come to be different.*

Opportunities come into view through a change of perspective. If you think only of safety and security, and not opportunity, then you close yourself off to possibilities.

This is why fear needs to be contained, if not conquered. Fear will cause you to retreat into your shell, and although you might be safe, you're also in the dark. Are you like that ship in the harbour that is safe but won't do what it is made for and sail forth over the horizon? Do you fear life more than death? Do you fear living more than dying?

If you're not willing to take a risk, then opportunity will pass you by like a helicopter taking off without you. So, like Walter Mitty, release your misgivings and use each opportunity to fly forth to your destiny.

3G #3: Your Opportunities Grow with Your Expectations

The first two attitudes of your 3G Network indicate something very important about opportunity:

> *Your opportunities have a direct relationship with your perspective.*

With attitude 3G #1: Your Opportunities are Unlimited in Number and Guise, your opportunities become more visible when you let go of your preconceptions of how they should appear. Problems are often opportunities in disguise. If you ignore your opportunities because of a hidden prejudice, they will go away.

With attitude 3G #2: Your Opportunities Are Your Personal Gift From Life, your opportunities wait for you to unwrap them and look inside. Like gifts with your name on them under the Christmas tree, you won't know what the present is until you give yourself permission to open them. If you are too scared to receive the gifts of Life, their joy will not be released.

So too with attitude 3G #3: Your Opportunities Grow with Your Expectations, your opportunities change as your attitude changes. The more you expect from Life, the more Life rewards you. As you grow, so do your opportunities. Or as Florence Scovel Shinn, author of the bestselling book, *The Game of Life and How to Play It*,[32] put it:

As you change, so do your opportunities.

You cannot grow beyond the limits you set yourself. You cannot grow in ability, character, knowledge, finances, or wisdom beyond the capabilities you set yourself.

As with the ancient custom of foot binding, you are shaped by your limitations. For centuries, despite the pain and the severe limitations to walking, Chinese aristocratic women subjected themselves and their daughters to the arduous process of foot binding. Petit bound feet were seen as cultured and desirable, and large unbound feet as uncultured and undesirable. The process itself meant breaking the bones of young girls' feet and then tightly binding them to shape and retard their size as the young girls grew into adulthood.

Foot binding is an example of the extreme lengths people will go to be admired and accepted in their community (and some would add, to keep women subjugated by men). But our expectations do the same thing. For whatever reasons we put these restrictions on ourselves, the result is the same as if we deliberately break our feet and tightly bind them—a painful, deformed, retarded, functionally useless, self-imposed limitation.

The point is, whether your expectations of yourself are high or low, they are the limits to which you can expand. This has a direct impact on how you see and make the most of your opportunities:

---

[32] *The Game of Life and How to Play It*, Florence Scovel Shinn, DeVorss, 1925

Your expectations of yourself set your opportunities.

Do you see yourself as a winner crossing the finishing line ahead of the pack? Or do you see yourself as lagging behind everyone else?

Do you want first prize in the Game of Life, or are you prepared to take a consolation prize? Does it matter if you live your dream, or is it not that important?

The answers to these questions reveal the expectations that you have for yourself. There's no right or wrong, but just be aware that your expectations are your limits, and you set your limits. Nobody else sets them—not society, not your teachers, not your parents, not your boss, not your partner—just you, and like tightly bounded feet you cannot grow beyond those self-imposed limits.

Thankfully, your limits aren't made of bone. You can change your attitude. You can change your expectations. You can change the limits you set for yourself.

Because your opportunities grow with your expectations.

CONVICTION: DEVOTING 100% TO YOUR DREAMS—I CAN

The next component of developing the Power Habit of Planning, Preparation & Perseverance and building the Power Element of Commitment is to devote 100% to your dreams. If we consider commitment as nothing more than the act that your intentions will be realised, once you have set your personal compass and consolidated your opportunities, the next step is to go all in and keep going until your dreams have been realised.

How you devote 100% to your dreams is by aligning your Attitude with your Imagination. In regard to commitment, this means to never give up on your dreams, to keep persevering toward your True North. This is best achieved through desire and dedication to your ultimate goal.

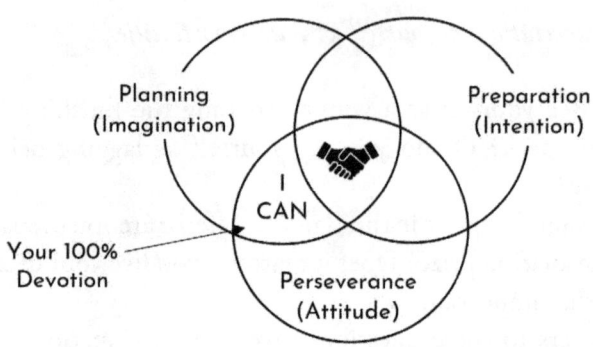

FIGURE 25: Your 100% Devotion–I Can

Those in The 5% Club know that you don't get something for nothing. They make full use of the Law of Cause and Effect, knowing that to get the effect they want they need to be the cause, and that usually entails hard work and effort. And for that, you need dedication.

You can't always control what's going on outside of you, but you can always control what's going on inside your mind, like your attitude and your commitment. So successful people work on what's going on inside as much or even more than what's going on outside. They work on what they can control, not what they can't control. They focus on controlling the controllables.

They focus on their Imagination, Intention, and Attitude.

Future Pacing and Desire

There is a school of thought that states there are no obstacles in life, only the lack of clarity of the path ahead. The only obstacles you face, therefore, are self-created. Your failure to see clearly, in other words. Your failure to focus. Your failure to remain undistracted.

As within, so without. A vague and cloudy idea of who you are, what you want, and how to get there is mirrored in your external world. The feeling that you're stuck in a rut, or you're going around and around in circles, is often the direct consequence of the lack of clarity. At core, it's a failure to utilise the Law of Cause and Effect to your benefit.

Remember, imagination is first cause, so that's the first thing you need to get right.

Like all superpowers, your Imagination must be trained. If you don't master your Imagination, your Imagination will master you. Up until now, your Imagination has probably been controlling you. We have all future paced our day. We have all anticipated what's ahead and made assumptions about how it will turn out. We have all done it, just not with any degree of conscious control or precision. Certainly not with the conscious control and precision of a professional Olympic athlete preparing for their gold medal event.

In *The Secret Life of Walter Mitty*, Walter Mitty has an extremely vivid imagination. He constructs an imaginary world in which he is various heroic and daring characters, such as an intrepid explorer coming to the rescue of Cheryl, or a master sculptor wooing his lover, most of which involve him having superpowers. But he uses his fantasy world to escape the humdrum of his real world. His imaginations aren't constructive, more flights of fancy than creative imaginings. They involve superhuman feats rather than down-to-earth human capabilities.

At least his imaginings have a good ending, usually with him saving the day. How often, though, do we imagine the opposite, that the worst will happen? How often do we anticipate that the outcome is going to be painful, or a burden, or just plainly unwanted? That the effort and cost we will need to put in and invest just isn't worth it?

We often use our Imagination superpower to project failure. We see ourselves unable to cross the finish line. We project an outcome we don't want more often than projecting an outcome we do want, and these negative forecasts are usually uncovered in the stories we tell ourselves.

"I'm not good enough."
"I don't deserve it."
"I always get things wrong."
"I'll never be able to afford it."
"What if I fail?"

Whilst still in primary school, my youngest daughter's netball team made it to the grand final, a remarkable feat considering the motley crew that had been assembled just a season before. But each girl had improved immensely since their first game, and they had developed into a tight little team punching way above their weight. They had already won two previous finals to progress to the grand final, and as I was driving my daughter to the game I could tell she was feeling nervous.

"What if I stuff up and we lose?" she said, visibly tense.

As the best player and linchpin of the team, she was putting a lot of pressure on herself to perform. Her low expectations were binding her. So I wanted her to visualise a better ending than the one she was currently projecting.

"What if you do well and win?" I replied.

This seemed to work, and as this new vision of doing well and winning, and not underperforming and losing the game, had a visible relaxing effect. Her change in attitude released her mental bindings and she was able to expand into her new, higher expectations. (As a side note, her team won the grand final by a single point against the top team in the competition.)

The upshot when we imagine or future pace an unwanted result is that we get filled with negative emotions based on those negative assumptions.

> *We end up reacting to something that hasn't yet happened, often with anxiety, worry, fear, and stress.*

We then bring that anxiety, worry, fear, and stress into our present moment. It affects our interactions with others and our relationships with them. It affects our energy levels and wellbeing. It affects the quality of our work and what we're doing.

This negative forecasting makes use of formula for success we've been using throughout this book, but to our detriment not our benefit. Let's use my daughter's grand final preparation as an example:

- -> Identity—a netballer who is not very good.
- -> Purpose—our team is probably going to lose.
- -> Conviction—I'm going to stuff up and not do very well.

This is not the best use of the formula for making the most of your opportunities and having fun. Each layer of thought is a layer of tight mental bindings, which, under such constrictions, you can't really hope to perform at your best.

But let's see how my daughter was able to change her negative forecast into a positive one:

- -> Identity—a netballer who is going to give it her best for the team.
- -> Purpose—our team can actually pull this off and win.
- -> Conviction—I'm going to play well and give 100% effort.

This is a better use of the formula for success. Each layer of thought is now a possibility into which you can grow and perform to your best.

Each layer of thought is how you can fuel your desire to live your dream.

Clarity and Dedication

Your thoughts are the ideas and concepts you want to see materialise and made real in the outside world. These are usually ideas and concepts of who you want to be, what you want to do, and how you are going to do it. If they are hazy and vague, the effect will be a direct reflection of those unclear thoughts and uncertain ideas.

Let's use the formula of success we've been using to explain how this works:

> -> Identity—I'm unsure; actually, I don't know.
>
> -> Purpose—well, I'm not sure exactly what I want to do.
>
> -> Conviction—to achieve what? I don't even know what I want to do.

By 2015, even though I had achieved a moderate amount of success, I reached a point where I felt as though I was going around and around in circles. I was doing a lot, but not getting the results I wanted in business and in my own writing. The 'hamster on the wheel' is a good analogy of my working day back then—running fast but not actually getting anywhere.

Each day was busy, very busy, usually starting with getting my daughters up for school, making their breakfast and lunch, driving them to school, then off to meetings, checking emails, and getting bogged in administration and paperwork for my business, DoctorZed Publishing. And all that by 11am.

Then it was writing my own books, developing workshops, creating online courses, blogging, tweeting, Facebooking, Instagramming, and any other social media platform I could find to promote my content.

Then it was editing manuscripts for clients, creating covers and interior layout design for books, converting books to ebooks, then distributing those books and ebooks to online platforms such as Amazon, Kobo, iTunes, Google Play, and hundreds of other retailers.

Then it was time to pick up the kids from school, take them to piano lessons, netball practice, netball games, singing, dancing, roller skating, swimming lessons, basketball practice, softball games, ice skating, and any other extracurricular activities they wanted to do.

Then it was rushing back home to cook dinner, wash the dishes, wash the clothes, dry the clothes, iron the clothes, put the garbage out, clean the gutters, mow the lawns, chop the firewood, water the garden, poison the weeds, help the kids with their homework, fix the trampoline, read bedtime stories, and prepare for the next day.

And that was just Monday!

I was like a human hamster seven days a week, 52 weeks a year. I did a lot but wasn't achieving a lot, especially with my personal goals, which I seemed to have pushed down the list of importance after family and business. I felt like a jigsaw puzzle scattered across the table, with lots of pieces to put together but no definite picture to work from.

I realised I needed to get a clearer picture of who I wanted to be, what I wanted to do, and how I was going to do it. I knew I wanted to be a writer, but I was struggling to find a common link connecting everything I was doing and to help me put all the pieces of the jigsaw together.

It was about this time that I realised where the problem was—with myself. Or more precisely, with my focus. I had inadvertently created obstacles on my path by focussing on the wrong things.

As a writer and storyteller at heart, my focus was obsessively on books. Books, books, books, books, books. I lived and breathed books. I thought constantly about books. Writing books was my first thought when I woke up in the morning, and my last thought when I went to bed at night. I wanted to be a bestselling author, I wanted to make a living from writing, and so books dominated my waking thoughts and my nighttime dreams.

But my obsessive focus on books had blinded me to the bigger picture. I thought books *were* the bigger picture, but they were only one piece of the puzzle. So, in effect, I had been trying in vain to complete the jigsaw picture using only one or two pieces of the puzzle.

As such, it was difficult to dedicate myself 100% to a grand vision because I wasn't really sure what I was dedicating myself to. In a moment of despair, I threw my hands in the air and grumbled to myself, "I don't know what to do anymore. Nothing I do seems to be working."

Then I remembered something a business coach once said to me in a workshop: "Think content, Scott. Content!"

Suddenly, as if the jigsaw box had been shaken and all the pieces fell out and laid into a completed picture, I saw how everything fitted together. Everything I was doing—books, ebooks, audiobooks, workshops, webinars, courses, online courses, coaching, mentoring, email marketing, newsletters, messaging, social media, video, podcasts, blogging—all slotted into place.

It was content I should be focussing on, not books. It was the underlying *message* of my content that was the glue that held all the pieces together. The books, ebooks, workshops, and all the other formats were just *platforms* for delivering my message. I had been focussing too much on the delivery method, not the content I wanted to be delivered. I had obsessed too much on the platform, not the message.

You see, there are readers who will never read my book, but they'll watch my video. There are clients who will never do my online courses, but they'll gladly attend a workshop. There are followers who will never listen to my podcasts, but they'll happily read my blog.

Same message, different platform.

I finally understood that it was the message that's important, not how the message was packaged, and my message to the world is simply this:

You already have what you're looking for. You already are that which you seek to be.

For a long time I had thought of myself as a writer where, in fact, I have always been a messenger. I saw myself as a storyteller, whereas storytelling was just my preferred platform for delivering my message. It could have been singing, or painting, or dancing, or acting, or any number of alternative platforms, but I had always been attracted to writing and storytelling as the means by which I wanted to get my message to the world.

My message is transformational. I am a messenger, delivering that transformational message through writing and storytelling. To clarify this important point, here's how everything I do fits together using the formula of success we're now familiar with:

- -> Identity—I am a transformational messenger.
- -> Purpose—to help humanity become an awakened species so that all can live with the abundance of joy, security, acceptance, peace, and freedom of our natural state of being.
- -> Conviction—to deliver my message through multiple platforms, such as books, ebooks, audiobooks, workshops, courses, coaching, mentoring, blogs, videos, podcasts, and social media.

Now I just have to roll up my sleeves and do it.

But having the clarity of who I am, what I want to achieve, why I do it, and how I can go about doing it, makes the path ahead so much clearer. When you have clarity, you can focus your thoughts and minimise distractions, thus removing many of those internal obstacles on your path to your chosen future. Having clarity also has another benefit:

> *Clarity makes it easier for you to commit to your path, and commitment helps you to keep moving forward and persevere.*

You might be able to see clearly ahead, but if you don't commit to your path you might give up when the going gets tough and stop before you cross the finish line.

A FINAL WORD ON COMMITMENT

It might surprise you to know that it's actually easier to be fully 100% committed to something than, say, being only 98% committed. Clayton Christensen, a former Harvard Business School professor, put it this way:

> *It's easier to hold your principles 100 percent of the time than it is to hold them 98 percent of the time.*

Let's use two imaginary characters, Jack and Jill, to illustrate this point. In this story, Jack and Jill don't need to climb a hill to fetch a pail of water, but they do want to eat healthier and lose a few winter kilograms for the upcoming summer.

Each decides on a healthy eating plan that they hope will achieve the results they're looking for. Jill decides on eating a lot more vegetables and salads, while Jack says he'll cut down on red meat and limit the amount of beer he's been drinking. Both diets will work if they commit to them and are disciplined in their eating habits. There's one big difference, however: Jill is 100% committed to her diet, whereas Jack is only 98% committed. Jill has invested her whole self into the outcome. Jack, not quite all.

Days 1-5 of their new diet go reasonably to plan. Jill is eating more salads and vegetables, and Jack has substituted red meat for chicken and has even cut down on his beer drinking in the evenings. However, the weekend approaches and they have been invited out for a Saturday evening barbeque by one of Jack's friends. The smell of barbequing T-bone steaks and burger patties greets them as they arrive at the house and begin to mingle with the other guests.

Jack's friend greets him with a slap on his back and thrusts a cold can of beer in his hands, saying, "What'll it be, Jack, T-bone or burger?"

Jack wavers a moment before replying, thinking to himself that it probably doesn't matter this one time if he doesn't follow his diet. "I'll have a T-bone, thanks," he says while taking a sip from the beer can, then adds, "medium rare, please."

Jill raises her eyebrows, and says, "What would your future self want you to do, Jack?"

But Jack doesn't have much connection to his future self, so he just shrugs and has another sip of beer. Jill shakes her head as she makes her way to the salad table, leaving Jack to face the consequences of his decisions.

What this story shows is something social psychologists have recognised since before the turn of the century, that events and situations often have greater influence over our behaviour than our desires. This is why many addicts return to their addiction after rehab if they go back to the environment in which they were using drugs or smoking cigarettes or drinking alcohol. They return to unhealthy habits in unhealthy environments.

The pull of our environment is often stronger than the pull of our willpower.

In our story, Jack is suffering from decision fatigue, which saps his willpower to stick to his diet. Because he has only committed himself 98% to eating less red meat and drinking less beer, he has opened the door to the odd occasion where he can break his own rules. Instead of slamming the door shut to those occasions, as Jill has, he is constantly questioning whether he should or shouldn't allow himself to eat red meat or to have another beer.

Jack has not yet learned to make a decision and then forget about it.

Should Jack encounter another situation where he is put in the spotlight to weigh what he should or shouldn't do, his willpower will most likely weaken further because the whole 'should I, shouldn't I?' decision-making process is mentally tiring and, if it goes on for long enough, mentally exhausting.

When this happens, it's much easier to give in to the situation than to keep fighting your mental battles. Then, like Jack, you justify your capitulation by claiming it doesn't really matter, or that you've done so well up until this moment you deserve a cheat day.

This is why it's much easier to be 100% committed to your principles than to be 98% committed to them. You don't suffer the mental exhaustion. You don't suffer the decision-fatigue. You don't allow the situation to overpower your willpower.

Because he is only partially committed to his new diet, Jack hasn't prepared himself for future scenarios where his resolve will be tested. He hasn't future paced himself, whereby he knows what outcome he wants or knows the behaviour required to persevere with his new eating plan.

Unlike Jill, who has worked through the outcome she wants in her mind for such occasions, Jack is only considering his present needs and is making decisions based on what his current self wants. Jill, though, because she feels connect to and responsible to her future self, often projects herself to the future she wants and considers how her future self would want to remember her current actions and behaviours and decisions.

She constantly asks herself the same question she posed earlier to Jack: "What would my future self want me to do?"

Jack doesn't have that 'future-self connection', so he doesn't ask this question. He therefore lacks the confidence and commitment he needs to adhere to his diet.

So it's no wonder he fails. He is kept from his goals not from external obstacles, but from internal obstacles created through his failure to commit 100% to his goal. Jill, on the other hand, has cleared her path to her goal through being 100% committed. She doesn't have the mental obstacles blocking her way because she can predict what she is going to do in future situations and knows the decisions she is going to make.

Because of her total commitment, Jill is able to persevere where Jack eventually gives up and relents.

Are You Jack Or Jill?

Being 100% committed to something is the ability to make a decision and then forgetting about it.

That means set and forget. Like cement.

Because he is only 98% committed, Jack's decisions aren't yet set. They're like wet cement, with no real form or strength. He can't build on them.

Jill's decisions, on the other hand, are set. Because she is 100% committed, they are like hard cement, with defined shape and great strength, a foundation upon which she can build and be confident that it will stand the test of time.

To help solidify your decision-making, consider the 7 Life Segments and the goals you might have set for each of them:

1. Family & Relationships: more time with your family, volunteering in your community, supporting your friends.
2. Career & Work: work/life balance, improving your skills, promotion, starting your own business.
3. Money & Finances: paying off your mortgage, starting a business, saving for retirement.
4. Health & Wellbeing: improving your fitness, working on your gratitude, having more peace of mind.
5. Learning & Education: learning a language or musical instrument, attending DIY courses, reading more books.
6. Fun & Adventure: reconnecting with nature, taking holidays, smiling more.
7. Spirituality & Ethics: being more mindful, focussing on big picture thinking, being more honest, Higher Self awareness.

Now consider your commitment to these goals. Are you Jack or Jill? Are you 98% or 100% committed to them? Because, as you now know:

The level of your commitment will determine the level of your achievement.

The level of your commitment will determine your membership to The 5% Club.

THE LAST WORD

THE SUPER ELEMENT

THE LAST WORD on success and happiness is, in fact, a reiteration of three words—Identity, Purpose, Conviction.

- -> Identity—I Am!
- -> Purpose—I Will!
- -> Conviction—I Can!

You now know the secret PIN to gain entry to The 5% Club. This secret PIN, of course, is the combination of the 4 Power Elements:

- -> *Faith*: the belief in who you are and what you do.
- -> *Valour*: the courage to live a life that's true to yourself.
- -> *Value*: the value you bring to others.
- -> *Commitment*: the investment of yourself into everything you do.

You have built each Power Element through its corresponding Power Habit:

- -> Power Habit #1: Self-Assuredness & Self-Belief has built the Power Element of *Faith*.
- -> Power Habit #2: Courage & Confidence has built the Power Element of *Valour*.
- -> Power Habit #3: Other People Thinking has built the Power Element of *Value*.
- -> Power Habit #4: Planning, Preparation & Perseverance has built the Power Element of *Commitment*.

These 4 Power Elements combine to create a Super Element:

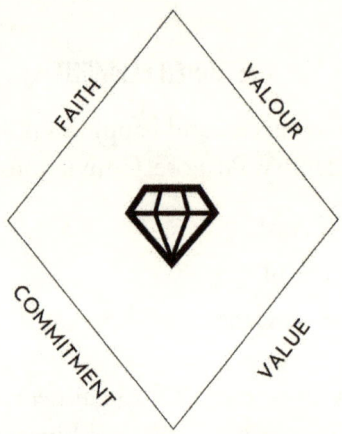

FIGURE 26: The Super Element

This Super Element is the key to manifesting the life you've always wanted. This Super Element, of course, is *Love*.

Love is alchemical: it transmutes failure into success.

Love is transformational: it transforms mediocrity into greatness.

Love is essential: it is what you are made of, the very essence of who you are.

Here, then, are the four steps to success and happiness:

1. Love *who* you are.
2. Love *what* you do.
3. Love *why* you do it.
4. Love *how* you do it.

When you love every aspect of who you are and what you do, when you express that love, there are no limits to what you can become. That's the power of love.

THE LAST WORD

Go now and reach for the stars. Have faith in who you are and your connection to the Universe and All That Is.

Stride forth with valour, and have the courage and confidence to live the life you want.

Know that you are of immense value to the world, that in fact you are a priceless gem, that without you this world is a lesser place.

Commit to being the person you were born to be, dedicate yourself 100% to your dreams and what you are capable of being.

Love who you are. Love what you do. Love why you do it. Love how you do it.

Love is your power, and that's the power of you.

* * *

If the content of this book contributes to your future success and happiness, I am delighted to have had some positive impact and I am grateful for the opportunity to help. If you would like to accelerate your journey, I'd be honoured to help you further. I have devoted myself to making the world a better place by helping others fulfil their immense potential and to make themselves better people.

Your success and happiness starts with you. If the difference between where you are now and what you are capable of being is how you think, then action is how you bridge the difference. I invite you now to reach out to me and join the growing community of Life Leaders who are committed to helping all of us become who we were born to be.

Don't let life pass by you—let life pass through you.

It's now up to you to help make this world a better place by being a better you.

You have that power.

FURTHER READING

The Strangest Secret: How to live the life you desire, Earl Nightingale, Nightingale Conant, 1957 (audio)

The Handbook to Higher Consciousness, Ken Keys Jr., Living Love Center, 1975

You Learn by Living: 11 Keys for a More Fulfilling Life, Eleanor Roosevelt, Harper, 1960

The Golden Chalice: A Pilgrim's Chronicle, Scott Zarcinas, DoctorZed Publishing, 2013

Think and Grow Rich, Napoleon Hill, The Ralston Society, 1937

Awakened Imagination and the Search, Neville Goddard, G. & J. Publishing, 1954

Secret Door to Success, Florence Scovel Shinn, DeVorss & Co., 1940

Man's Search for Meaning, Viktor Frankl, Beacon Press, 1959 (first published 1946, Austria)

The Road Less Travelled: A New Psychology of Love, Traditional Values and Spiritual Growth, M. Scott Peck, Simon and Schuster, 1978

Zen Mind, Beginner's Mind, Shunryu Suzuki, Weatherhill, 1970

As a Man Thinketh, James Allen, D. MacKay Co., 1890

See You At The Top, Zig Ziglar, Pelican Publishing Co., 1974

Zen and the Art of Motorcycle Maintenance: An Inquiry into Values, Robert Pirsig, William Morrow & Co., 1974

Eat that Frog!, Brian Tracey, Berrett-Koehler, 2001

FURTHER READING

The Alchemist, Paulo Coelho, HarperSanFrancisco (HarperOne), 1988

Being YOU! Awaken to the Abundance of Your Natural State of Being, Scott Zarcinas, DoctorZed Publishing, 2023

The Magic of Thinking Big, David J. Schwartz, Wilshire Book Co., 1959

The Keys to Success, Jim Rohn, Brolga Publishing, 2002

The Gifts of Imperfection: Let Go of Who You Think You're Supposed to Be and Embrace Who You Are, Brené Brown, Hazelden, 2010

The Science of Getting Rich, Wallace D. Wattles, Elizabeth Towne Co., 1910

Samantha Honeycomb: A Pilgrim's Chronicle, Scott Zarcinas, DoctorZed Publishing, 2006

The Game of Life and How to Play It, Florence Scovel Shinn, DeVorss, 1925

Connect with DoctorZed

Facebook: YNSOB.by.Dr.Scott.Zarcinas
LinkedIn: dr-scott-zarcinas-6572399
Instagram: doctorzed_motivational_speaker
Twitter: @DrScottZarcinas
Website: *scottzarcinas.com*

Growing great people is how you grow a great business!	*The Life You Want, the Way You Want, How You Want!*
Are you a leader of a team, involved in a team environment, a business owner, or entrepreneur looking to grow your business?	Looking for a coach or mentor to help you get direction and take your life to the next level?
Ask me how I can help your business grow by growing your people.	Ask me how I can help you maximise your capabilities and reach your fullest potential.
E: scott.zarcinas@doctorzed.com W: scottzarcinas.com/contact	E: scott.zarcinas@doctorzed.com W: scottzarcinas.com/contact

Book DoctorZed for Your Next Function!
Keynotes • MC • Presentations

scottzarcinas.com/book-doctorzed/

Other Titles by Scott Zarcinas

Being YOU! Awaken to the Abundance of Your Natural State of Being
by Scott Zarcinas M.D.

ISBN: 978-0-6456384-8-6
eISBN: 978-0-6456384-9-3

DoctorZed Publishing

Available in print and ebook.

'Refreshing. A tonic to read. Comprehensive and scholarly, it also has so many poetic qualities.'
~ Roger Rees, Emeritus Professor of Disability Studies and Research, Flinders University

You already have what you are looking for!

Ever wanted the answers to life's deepest questions: Who am I? Why do I do what I do? What am I doing with my life?

When you awaken to the abundance of your natural state of being, you will get to the heart of the motivating forces and innermost needs of your life.

But unlike 'quick fix' and 'step-by-step' guides, this book offers real solutions to living a life of abundance through the understanding of your true self.

www.scottzarcinas.com/books/being-you

The Banana Trap: How to Escape a Life of Stress and Finally Break Free
by Scott Zarcinas M.D.

ISBN: 978-0-6485726-1-9
eISBN: 978-0-6487107-9-0

DoctorZed Publishing

Available in print and ebook.

Science-based Stress Management Strategies to De-Stress & Prosper

Do you feel overwhelmed and over-stressed? Are you trapped in recurring cycles of worry and frustration? Do you crumble in stressful moments?

Don't worry, everybody has moments of high stress and overwhelm! This guidebook will help you to:

- Feel less overwhelmed and more confident.
- Escape The Banana Trap and reclaim your life.
- Identify and overcome the different types of stress.
- Eliminate stressful habits and increase happiness.
- Deal with high-pressure situations and be in control.

PLUS develop a long-term strategy to prevent high stress before it occurs.

www.scottzarcinas.com/books/the-banana-trap

It's Up to YOU! Why Most People Fail to Live the Life they Want and How to Change It
by Scott Zarcinas M.D.

ISBN: 978-0-6485726-4-0
eISBN: 978-0-6485726-3-3

DoctorZed Publishing

Available in print and ebook.

Featuring 9 Life Leadership Strategies to Live the Life You Want, the Way You Want, How You Want.

Do you feel stuck in a rut and your life is on hold? Are you looking for new direction but don't know which way to turn?

We all want to do more than just survive; we want to thrive. But if you're trapped in the same old routine, now is the time to start living the life you were born to live—with abundance.

This book is your go-to manual if:

- You need a break from the old and to take a new direction.
- You desire greater success and fulfillment.
- You seek the confidence to be yourself and not what others expect you to be.

www.scottzarcinas.com/books/its-up-to-you

www.ingramcontent.com/pod-product-compliance
Lightning Source LLC
LaVergne TN
LVHW040115080426
835507LV00039B/179